YANKEE MAGAZINE'S
Lost and Vintage Recipes

YANKEE MAGAZINE'S

Lost and Vintage Recipes

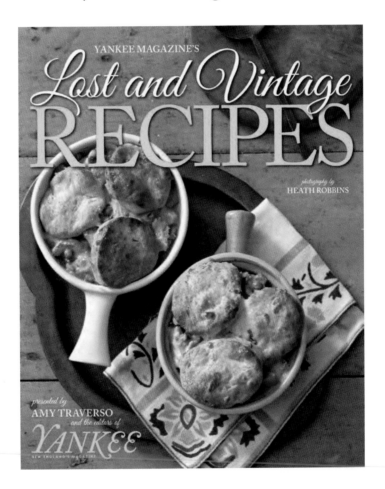

compiled and edited by Amy Traverso,
Senior Lifestyle Editor, *Yankee Magazine*

Book design by Lori Pedrick and Jill Shaffer Hammond
Composition by Lori Pedrick and Jill Shaffer Hammond
Photography by Heath Robbins
Food styling by Catrine Kelty
Prop styling by Beth Wickwire/Ennis Inc.
Props and linens supplied by
    Twin Elm Farm, *133 Wilton Road, Peterborough, NH 03458*;
    White Home Collections, *9 Greenville Road, Wilton, NH 03086*;
    and Bower Bird, *16 Depot St. #60, Peterborough, NH 03458*

Published by The Countryman Press, P.O. Box 748, Woodstock, VT 05091
Distributed by W. W. Norton & Company, Inc., 500 Fifth Avenue, New York, NY 10110
Printed in the United States of America

10 9 8 7 6 5 4 3 2 1

Library of Congress Cataloging-in-Publication Data are available

Yankee Magazine's Lost and Vintage Recipes
978-1-58157-181-3

For the generations
of home cooks
who came before us
and whose recipes
still inspire us today

Recipe Index

Introduction

Recipes tell a story. Not in the familiar sense—there are no plot points in the ingredients list, no surprise endings in the method (except, maybe, when it comes to soufflés). But if you step back and look at recipes over time and as a whole, they tell a rich story about how people lived: how, for example, the invention of jet airliners and the post-war economic boom combined with the efforts of a Cambridge cookbook author named Julia Child to bring about an interest in French cooking—which, in turn, made fondue and crêpes Suzette the go-to foods for entertaining in the 1960s.

They also teach us about how times change and how fashions fall away. Remember chicken Kiev? Blueberry "boy bait"? Fondue? These recipes were blockbusters in their day, but were eventually replaced by the next food fad or dietary restriction. Some were forgotten for good reason. When's the last time you craved jellied bean salad or deviled egg casserole? But anyone who grew up eating made-from-scratch cheese straws, chicken pot pie, Joe Froggers, or stack cake remembers them, even if the recipes have been lost to time. And they're well worth revisiting.

That's what inspired us to spend time scouring *Yankee*'s archive of 75-plus years of food stories in search of "lost" and vintage recipes worthy of revival. These archives are one of the great joys of working for a magazine as old and as storied as ours. In the second-floor conference room of our headquarters in Dublin, New Hampshire, we have a leather-bound record of how New Englanders have lived since our first issue was published by Robb Sagendorph in 1935. We can see not only how tastes have changed but also how recipes themselves have morphed from rough sketches ("Make a pastry as for pie, fill with a chicken that has been poached with carrots and onion as for soup. Add cream as needed to make a gravy and season to taste . . .") to the highly specific, standardized form we use today. We browsed our recipes, looked for examples that sparked our imaginations, and then retested and tweaked them as needed to appeal more to contemporary tastes. In some places, we cut out a bit of fat or replaced prepared foods (such as canned cream of mushroom soup) with from-scratch ingredients—but we stayed true to the spirit of these dishes.

In many cases we were reminded that earlier cooks had some brilliant tricks up their sleeves that we today seem to have forgotten. For example, why did we all stop using sherry, port, vermouth, and brandy in our cooking? They add wonderful depth of flavor to our chicken à la king, turkey Tetrazzini, and baked scallops. Also, homemade sauces really do taste so much better than store-bought—and take hardly any time at all. Buttermilk dressing, hot fudge sauce, and butterscotch sauce are well within the means of any busy home cook, and spending 10 minutes to prepare them will take your cooking to a new level. Finally, it's worth noting that while our mothers and grandmothers were making rich dishes such as beef Stroganoff, Swedish meatballs, and potato doughnuts for their families, they did so without creating a national obesity epidemic. We needn't fear delicious foods like these—but, rather, we can enjoy them in moderation and in reasonable portion sizes.

Cooking these foods brought back happy memories of our own family dinner tables and reminded us that what's old can be great again. We hope you'll enjoy this book as much as we've enjoyed working on it.

—*Amy Traverso,*
Senior Lifestyle Editor, Yankee Magazine

ACKNOWLEDGMENTS

I'd like to thank all the people who worked to produce *Yankee Magazine's Lost and Vintage Recipes*: designer Jill Shaffer Hammond, art director Lori Pedrick, associate editor Aimee Seavey, managing editor Eileen Terrill, copy editor Lida Stinchfield, photographer Heath Robbins, food stylist Catrine Kelty, prop stylist Beth Wickwire, photo editor Heather Marcus, senior production artist Lucille Rines, production director Dave Ziarnowski, and recipe testers Kristen Widican and Andy Clurfeld. —*A. T.*

Enjoy!

Pantry Notes

BUTTER

Many pastry chefs eschew salted butter, arguing that the unsalted variety has purer flavor and higher fat content, which is better for piecrust and pastry. We agree, but in cases where the fat content doesn't make a significant difference, as with brownies, cookies, and muffins, we decided to spare you the extra trip to the grocery store, and so those recipes call for salted butter instead. For brands, we like Kate's of Maine *(kateshome madebutter.com)*, Cabot *(cabotcheese.coop)*, and Vermont Butter & Cheese Creamery *(vermontcreamery.com)*.

BUTTERMILK

Buttermilk may sound old-fashioned, but it adds wonderful flavor to many baked goods. The acid in the milk also relaxes the gluten in the flour, making dough more tender. And it's still sold at almost every supermarket. Low-fat buttermilk is a better choice for baking than fat-free, but if the latter is your only option, you may use them interchangeably. And if you don't have any buttermilk at all, you can add a tablespoon of lemon juice or mild vinegar to a cup of milk, let it sit for 10 minutes, and then use it in place of buttermilk.

COCOA POWDER

There are two kinds of unsweetened cocoa powder available today: Dutch-process and natural. The former is treated with an alkalizing agent to neutralize its acids. Because it's less acidic, Dutch-process cocoa tends to be paired with baking powder as the leavening agent in cakes and pastries. It has a milder flavor and dissolves well in liquids. Most of the common Dutch-process brands, such as Lindt, Droste, and Valrhona, are European in origin. Natural cocoa powder has a stronger, rather bitter flavor and will react with baking soda, thanks to its acidity. It's often used in more rustic pastries, such as brownies and cookies, although some cakes do call for it. Popular American brands such as Hershey, Ghirardelli, and Scharffen Berger are natural cocoa products.

EGGS

Most recipes in this book call for large eggs, except where otherwise noted. White or brown (or blue or green) eggs are all fine, and, as always, we recommend buying local! (See "The Well-Tempered Egg," p. 181, for a tip on how to prevent eggs from curdling in sauces, soups, and confections.)

FLOUR

The majority of the recipes in this book call for all-purpose flour, except for some cakes that benefit from the lighter qualities of cake flour. For both of these types, as New Englanders we can't help but recommend Vermont's own King Arthur brand *(king arthurflour.com)*. For whole-grain flours, we also love the ones grown and milled by the L'Etoile family of Four Star Farms of Northfield, Massachusetts *(four starfarms.com)*.

MILK

Unless otherwise noted, you may use whatever milk you happen to have on hand in these recipes.

SALT

For cooking, we tend to prefer kosher salt. It's easy to sprinkle and seems to have a slightly "cleaner" flavor than iodized (table) salt. However, for finer-grained cakes and pastries where sifting is required or texture is an issue, we call for table salt. If you don't happen to have any kosher salt on hand, you can substitute table salt—just use half the recommended amount.

VEGETABLE OIL

If a recipe calls for vegetable oil, feel free to use corn, safflower, canola, walnut, grapeseed, or any other type of mild oil you have on hand. Olive oil also works, but the extra-virgin type can add a recognizable flavor to baked goods—not necessarily a bad thing, but something to keep in mind.

CHEESE STRAWS,
BLUE CHEESE BISCUITS,
MARJORIE'S GREEN TOMATO RELISH
(recipes on pages 19, 18, 162)

Appetizers

If classic cocktails are enjoying a long revival, then it's high time to revisit the vintage appetizers and hors d'oeuvres that are just made for nibbling with drinks (or, for that matter, without). Our recipes for gougères, cheese straws, and deviled eggs are ripe for rediscovery, while blue cheese biscuits, soda crackers, and pâté bring a little extra joy to happy hour. For seafood lovers, crab farci, and oysters Rockefeller are favorite ways to begin a meal.

CLASSIC DEVILED EGGS

TOTAL TIME: 55 MINUTES • HANDS-ON TIME: 25 MINUTES • YIELD: 6 EGGS

8 large eggs, hard-boiled
3–4 tablespoons mayonnaise
2 teaspoons Dijon mustard
¼ teaspoon cayenne pepper
2 tablespoons minced celery (optional)
2 tablespoons minced red onion (optional)
Kosher or sea salt and freshly ground black pepper, to taste
Garnishes: paprika, chives (optional)

1. Slice hard-boiled eggs in half lengthwise, carefully remove the yolks, and transfer yolks to a bowl. Set whites aside.
2. Using a fork or pastry cutter, mash the yolks. Add mayonnaise, mustard, cayenne pepper, celery, onion, salt, and black pepper to taste.
3. Spoon the filling into a zip-top bag, cut off a corner tip, and then pipe into the egg-white halves. Garnish with paprika and chives if you like. Chill and serve.

CRAB *FARCI* DIP

In French, the word farci *means "stuffed," and* crabe farci *is a popular French appetizer in which the shells are stuffed with a mix of crabmeat, breadcrumbs, butter, and seasonings. Like New England's own baked stuffed lobster, crab* farci *has many variations—the dish also appears in Cajun, Caribbean, and Vietnamese cooking—but in this version, it's translated into an easy, delicious dip to serve with crackers or thin slices of French bread.*

TOTAL TIME: 45 MINUTES • HANDS-ON TIME: 15 MINUTES • YIELD: 5 SERVINGS

Salted butter (for baking dish)
3 tablespoons salted butter, melted
¾ cup dry plain breadcrumbs
½ teaspoon kosher or sea salt
1 can (6 ounces) crabmeat, drained and shredded
½ cup heavy cream
1 scant teaspoon minced shallot or onion
2 tablespoons freshly squeezed lemon juice
¼ teaspoon freshly ground black pepper
Garnishes: lemon wedges, fresh parsley sprigs or fresh thyme (optional)

1. Preheat the oven to 350°. Lightly butter a small baking dish and set aside.
2. In a small bowl, stir together the melted butter, breadcrumbs, and salt. Set aside about half of this mixture for the topping. Combine the rest with the crabmeat, cream, shallot or onion, lemon juice, and pepper.
3. Spoon the mixture into the baking dish, top with the reserved breadcrumbs, and bake until golden and bubbling, 20 to 30 minutes. Serve hot, garnished with lemon and parsley or thyme if you like.

CLASSIC DEVILED EGGS
(recipe on opposite page)

CHEDDAR GOUGÈRES

Knowing how to make a quick batch of these airy cheese puffs is one of the best skills a hostess can acquire. They're so simple, and they always get a big reaction from guests—especially when made with sharp Vermont cheddar cheese. Cambridge's own Julia Child popularized them in her book Mastering the Art of French Cooking, *and we feel it's time for a gougères revival!*

TOTAL TIME: 55 MINUTES • **HANDS-ON TIME:** 25 MINUTES • **YIELD:** ABOUT 40 PUFFS

8 tablespoons (1 stick) salted butter
1 cup water
1 cup all-purpose flour
5 large eggs
1½ cups grated extra-sharp cheddar cheese
⅛ teaspoon freshly grated nutmeg
1 teaspoon freshly ground black pepper

1. Preheat the oven to 425°. Line two baking sheets with parchment paper. Warm butter and water in a medium-size saucepan over medium-high heat until butter is melted and the mixture comes to a low boil.

2. Turn heat to low, add flour, and stir vigorously until the mixture coheres and pulls away from the sides of the pan, about 1 minute. Remove pan from heat.

3. Add eggs, one at a time, stirring vigorously after each. Dough will separate after each addition; keep stirring until it forms a smooth paste. Stir in cheese, nutmeg, and pepper. (The dough should still be hot enough to melt the cheese.)

4. Drop the mixture by the heaping teaspoonful onto the baking sheet. (For a prettier presentation, you can pipe the batter into 1¼-inch mounds.) Bake until puffed and brown, about 30 minutes. For extra-crisp puffs, pierce each one with a knife; then turn off the oven and put the puffs back in for 10 minutes.

LOST AND VINTAGE RECIPES

Appetizers

CHICKEN LIVER PÂTÉ

Pâté, once an entertaining staple, is generally thought of as a luxury item today, which seems silly once you realize how easy (and inexpensive) it is to make. Plus it freezes beautifully for months, so you can keep it on hand for surprise holiday guests.

Make-ahead tip: You may freeze the pâté after cooling: Divide among individual ramekins (for easy serving), wrap each one first in plastic and then in aluminum foil, and freeze. Or store in the refrigerator for up to 5 days.

TOTAL TIME: 45 MINUTES · **HANDS-ON TIME:** 45 MINUTES · **YIELD:** ABOUT 3 CUPS

3	**slices bacon**
1	**medium-size yellow onion, diced**
2	**medium-size carrots, grated**
2	**large cloves garlic, minced**
3	**tablespoons salted butter**
1	**pound chicken livers (preferably organic), trimmed of fat and rinsed**
2	**tablespoons brandy or port wine**
1½	**teaspoons kosher or sea salt**
¾	**teaspoon freshly ground black pepper**
¼	**teaspoon grated nutmeg**
½	**cup chopped fresh parsley, plus more for garnish**
¼–½	**cup heavy cream (optional)**

1. In a large skillet, cook bacon over moderate heat until browned. Add onion and continue cooking until golden. Add carrots, garlic, and butter; cook until carrots are tender.

2. Remove the pan from the heat and add chicken livers and brandy or port. Return the pan to the heat and cook, stirring gently, until livers are cooked through but slightly pink in the center, 6 to 8 minutes. Season with salt, pepper, and nutmeg. Add parsley and stir; then remove from heat, put into a food processor, and process until smooth. If you like a creamier consistency, add cream.

3. Serve garnished with parsley on a platter surrounded by crackers, sliced French bread, gherkins, onions, and capers, if you like.

BLUE CHEESE BISCUITS

Searching Yankee's *archives for appetizers from the 1930s, 1940s, and 1950s, we came across a number of recipes that featured Roquefort cheese as a star ingredient: in dressing, in cheese balls, in a jellied mousse (we declined to test that one). We were especially drawn to a biscuit recipe that used tangy Roquefort as an accent to balance the dough's buttery richness. The biscuits were a winner, and we were inspired to update them by using local cheeses in the recipe. Serve with slices of good ham, a drizzle of honey or the green-tomato relish on p. 162, or a smear of extra blue cheese and some walnuts.*

TOTAL TIME: 40 MINUTES • **HANDS-ON TIME:** 15 MINUTES • **YIELD:** 16 TWO-INCH BISCUITS

NOTE: *You can use Roquefort or any good blue cheese in these biscuits, but we especially recommend local varieties like Great Hill Blue, made in Marion, Massachusetts, or Bayley Hazen Blue from Jasper Hill Farm in Greensboro, Vermont.*

1¾ **cups all-purpose flour, plus more for work surface**
1 **tablespoon baking powder**
1 **teaspoon table salt**
¼ **cup blue cheese, crumbled (see "Note," above)**
¼ **cup cold unsalted butter, cut into small cubes, plus more for pan**
⅔ **cup milk**

1. Preheat the oven to 425°. Line a baking sheet with parchment paper or grease with butter.
2. In a medium-size bowl, whisk together the flour, baking powder, and salt. Transfer to your freezer for 10 minutes to let everything get cold.
3. Take the bowl from the freezer and use a pastry cutter to work the cheese and butter into the flour mixture until it looks like coarse sand with pea-sized lumps (see p. 181, bottom). Slowly add milk, stirring with a fork as you go, until mixture just holds together.
4. Turn the dough out onto a floured surface, knead three times, and gently press out to a ½-inch thickness. Use a floured biscuit cutter or 2-inch glass rim to cut the biscuits out, gathering and rerolling the dough as needed. Arrange biscuits on the baking sheet and bake until golden brown and fragrant, 12 to 15 minutes.

CHEESE STRAWS

Cheese-based hors d'oeuvres have always been a New England mainstay, particularly during the era that we now consider "vintage." They're tasty, salty enough to whet your thirst, and rich enough to feel substantial. These cheese straws can trace their roots back to France and later England, where puffed-pastry rounds sprinkled with cheese were called "Sefton fancies."

TOTAL TIME: 30 MINUTES • HANDS-ON TIME: 20 MINUTES • YIELD: ABOUT 2 DOZEN

1 **cup all-purpose flour, plus more for work surface**
¼ **teaspoon table salt**
½ **cup (1 stick) cold unsalted butter,**
      cut into small cubes,
      plus more for baking sheets
1 **cup sharp cheddar cheese, grated, divided**
3 **tablespoons very cold water**
      Dash Tabasco

1. Preheat the oven to 400° and grease two baking sheets.
2. In a large bowl, whisk together flour and salt. Using your fingers or a pastry blender, work the butter and half the cheese into the flour (see p. 181, bottom). Add water and Tabasco; then turn the dough out onto a floured board and lightly knead in the remaining cheese until the dough comes together.
3. Roll the dough into a ¼-inch-thick rectangle; then cut into strips ½ inch wide and 5 inches long. Arrange the strips on the prepared baking sheets, and bake until nicely browned, 10 to 12 minutes. Serve warm or at room temperature.

OLD-FASHIONED SODA CRACKERS

TOTAL TIME: 40 MINUTES · HANDS-ON TIME: 30 MINUTES · YIELD: 40 TO 50 CRACKERS

2½ cups all-purpose flour, plus more for work surface
    and rolling dough
½ teaspoon baking soda
½ teaspoon kosher or sea salt
3 tablespoons cold unsalted butter, cut into small cubes
1 cup whole milk
    Kosher or sea salt

1. Preheat the oven to 375° and line two baking sheets with parchment.
2. In a large bowl, whisk together the flour, baking soda, and salt. Add the cold butter, working it into the dry ingredients with your fingers until it resembles coarse meal.
3. Add the milk slowly and mix the dough gently; then knead it, until it just comes together and is tacky but not sticky. (If necessary, add more flour.) Wrap in plastic and refrigerate for 1 hour.
4. Turn the dough out onto a floured surface. Divide in half, and return one half to the refrigerator. Roll out the other half ⅛ inch thick, sprinkling with more flour as needed to prevent sticking. Use a pizza cutter to cut it into 2-inch squares.
5. Transfer the squares to the baking sheets, leaving an inch of space between them; then sprinkle with salt, and prick them all over with a fork.
6. Bake until golden brown and crisp, about 15 minutes, depending on size.
7. Repeat with the second half of the dough.

OYSTERS ROCKEFELLER

This classic New Orleans dish, circa 1899, gets a fresh spin with tarragon and shallots replacing the usual parsley and garlic. It gets its New England accent from a topping of buttery Ritz cracker crumbs (whose predecessor was invented in Newburyport, Massachusetts). To save time, ask your fishmonger to shuck the oysters, but be sure to save their precious liquor (juices).

TOTAL TIME: 55 MINUTES • **HANDS-ON TIME:** 45 MINUTES • **YIELD:** 6 TO 10 SERVINGS

1	**sleeve of Ritz crackers, crushed**
4	**tablespoons unsalted butter, melted**
2	**tablespoons cold unsalted butter**
2	**medium-size shallots, minced**
¼	**cup Pernod liqueur**
2	**cups heavy cream**
1	**teaspoon fresh tarragon leaves**
2	**cups roughly chopped fresh baby spinach leaves, firmly packed**
1	**tablespoon freshly grated Parmigiano-Reggiano**
20	**medium-size Atlantic oysters**
	Kosher or sea salt and freshly ground black pepper, to taste

1. Preheat the oven to 425°. Line a baking sheet with an extra-long piece of aluminum foil; then bunch the foil up in spots to create 20 small wells, which will hold the oysters and keep them upright.

2. Make the topping: In a medium-size bowl, stir together the crushed crackers and 4 tablespoons melted butter. Set aside.

3. In a medium-size saucepan over medium-high heat, melt 2 tablespoons butter. Add the shallots and cook until translucent, about 4 minutes. Remove the pan from the heat and add Pernod. Return the pan to the heat and bring the liquid to a simmer. Once simmering, remove the pan from the heat again and use a match to ignite the liquid, letting the alcohol burn off for 10 to 15 seconds (the flames will subside on their own).

4. Add the cream and tarragon, bring to a simmer, and cook until reduced by half, about 10 minutes. Add the spinach and cook, stirring, until wilted. Remove the pan from the heat, stir in the cheese, and let stand until cool.

5. Meanwhile, shuck the oysters, preserving their liquor (juices) in the shells. Nestle the shells in foil on the prepared baking sheet. Add 1 tablespoon sauce to each oyster and sprinkle with 1 tablespoon of the cracker mixture. Bake until the sauce is bubbling and the topping is golden brown, about 5 minutes. Season with salt and pepper to taste.

CORN CHOWDER
(recipe on page 19)

Soups and Salads

American salads have come a long way since the days of carrot gelatin molds, but if you've never tasted the wonders of fresh Harvard beets, caraway coleslaw, or our updated take on Waldorf salad (made with chicken, for a full meal), you're in for a treat. Serve with our fresh cream of mushroom soup, corn chowder, or lobster bisque, and you have a feast.

AROOSTOOK POTATO & BROCCOLI SOUP
(recipe on opposite page)

AROOSTOOK POTATO & BROCCOLI SOUP

Aroostook County in Maine is potato country, and for generations the local cooks have devised ingenious ways to use their fine spuds. Potato soups and chowders are one popular way. Use Maine potatoes, cheddar from Vermont, and broccoli from a local farm to make this brawny soup into an all-star New England supper. Garnish with more coarsely grated cheddar and serve with brown bread.

TOTAL TIME: 55 MINUTES • **HANDS-ON TIME:** 25 MINUTES • **YIELD:** 4 TO 6 SERVINGS

6 **cups russet or Yukon Gold potatoes, peeled and cut into 2-inch chunks**

4 **cups chopped broccoli florets and thinly sliced stems**

4 **cups reduced-sodium chicken broth**

1 **cup whole milk**

2 **cups grated sharp cheddar cheese, plus more for garnish**

Kosher or sea salt and freshly ground black pepper, to taste

1. Put potatoes in a 4- to 5-quart heavy-bottomed pot and cover with water. Set the pot on the stovetop over high heat and bring to a boil. Reduce heat to low, cover, and simmer until tender, about 15 minutes. When done, drain potatoes. Mash half the potatoes; set aside both the mashed potatoes and the potato chunks.

2. Put the broccoli in the soup pot and add the chicken broth. Bring to a boil over high heat; then reduce heat to low and simmer until broccoli is tender, 6 to 7 minutes. Remove from heat and cool slightly.

3. Working in batches, purée the broccoli/broth mixture in a blender with the potato chunks. Return the purée to the soup pot, set over medium heat, and stir in the mashed potatoes and milk; let warm for 2 minutes. Stir in the cheddar, and when it's well blended, about 3 minutes, season to taste with salt and pepper. Serve garnished with additional grated cheddar.

LOBSTER BISQUE

A lobster could hardly hope to meet a more glorious end—a wonderful way to highlight the deliciousness of a single ingredient.

TOTAL TIME: 1 HOUR 10 MINUTES • **HANDS-ON TIME:** 40 MINUTES • **YIELD:** 6 TO 8 SERVINGS

¾–1 **pound cooked lobster meat, in whole pieces (claws, tails, etc.)**

3 **tablespoons salted butter**

1 **small onion, minced**

2 **medium-size carrots, shredded**

3 **plum tomatoes, peeled and chopped**

2½ **teaspoons kosher or sea salt, plus more to taste**

¼ **teaspoon freshly ground black or white pepper**

¾ **cup dry white wine, such as Pinot Grigio**

3½ **cups fish broth or water**

¾ **cup light cream**

2 **egg yolks, lightly beaten**

2 **tablespoons brandy**

   Garnishes: reserved lobster-claw meat and chopped chervil, basil, or parsley

1. Set aside the best-looking claw piece for the garnish. Chop the rest of the meat and set aside.

2. In a 4- to 5-quart heavy-bottomed pot over medium heat, melt butter and cook onion, carrots, tomatoes, salt, and pepper until onions are translucent, about 6 minutes. Add the chopped meat, wine, and fish broth or water. Bring to a boil; then cover, reduce heat to low, and simmer 30 minutes. Purée mixture in batches in an electric blender until completely smooth (this may take a few minutes). Rinse out the saucepan to remove any solids, and return to low heat.

3. Pour the purée back into the pot. (For the smoothest texture, pass purée through a fine-mesh sieve.) Stir in cream and heat for about 5 minutes. Put the beaten egg yolks in a small bowl. Slowly add about ¼ cup of the hot soup mixture, whisking continuously (see p. 181, top). Add a bit more soup, whisking again. Pour the mixture back into the pan, stirring continuously, and heat gently until slightly thickened. Add brandy and more salt to taste. Serve warm, garnished with reserved lobster meat and herbs.

LOBSTER BISQUE
(recipe on opposite page)

ALMOND SOUP

The almond has been a treasured ingredient as long as recorded history. It played an important role in early Arab and medieval cooking, and long before chefs learned to use roux or eggs to thicken their soups and sauces, they used bread and nuts. Traditional almond soups, rich with garlic, are still common in Spain, but this creamy version has a more 20th-century American profile. It's delicious and unexpected.

TOTAL TIME: 40 MINUTES • **HANDS-ON TIME:** 25 MINUTES • **YIELD:** 6 SERVINGS

1½ cups blanched slivered almonds
4 tablespoons salted butter
1 shallot, minced
¼ cup all-purpose flour
4 cups reduced-sodium chicken broth
1 tablespoon fresh lemon juice
1 tablespoon granulated sugar
1 teaspoon kosher or sea salt
¼ teaspoon freshly ground black pepper
½ cup light cream
2 teaspoons minced fresh tarragon or chervil, plus more for garnish
½ teaspoon almond extract (optional)

1. In a 4- to 5-quart heavy-bottomed pot over low heat, toast the nuts until nicely browned, 5 to 7 minutes. Transfer to a bowl. Return the pot to medium heat, melt the butter, and add the minced shallot. Cook until translucent, about 2 minutes. Add the flour and stir until glossy, about 3 minutes. Add the toasted almonds, broth, lemon juice, sugar, salt, and pepper. Reduce heat to medium-low and cook, stirring occasionally, for 15 minutes.

2. In a blender, purée the soup in batches until smooth (this may take a few minutes); then return it to the stove and add the cream, tarragon (or chervil), and, if you like, almond extract. Serve garnished with additional tarragon (or chervil).

CHESTNUT SOUP WITH BACON

Chestnut soup, chestnut dressing, chestnut desserts—all remind us of the British roots of many traditional Yankee favorites. Make this hearty soup part of your everyday repertoire by using preroasted, vacuum-packed chestnuts.

TOTAL TIME: 50 MINUTES • **HANDS-ON TIME:** 30 MINUTES • **YIELD:** 6 SERVINGS

NOTE: *Using preroasted, vacuum-packed chestnuts sold in glass jars makes this soup incredibly easy. Look for them in supermarkets during the holidays and in most gourmet and Whole Foods stores year-round (a warning, though: they can be expensive off-season). Don't use the canned type, which generally lack flavor. To roast chestnuts yourself, cut an X through the flat bottom of each nut (this helps with peeling later). Toss chestnuts with salt, pepper, and ⅓ cup canola oil. Spread on a baking sheet and roast at 425° until tender, 25 to 35 minutes. Return chestnuts to the bowl, toss, and cover bowl with plastic wrap. Cool, then peel.*

- 4 **slices bacon**
- 1 **tablespoon olive oil**
- 1 **medium-size red onion, coarsely chopped**
- 1 **celery stalk, coarsely chopped**
- 2 **medium-size carrots, peeled and coarsely chopped**
- 1 **large tart apple, such as Granny Smith, peeled, cored, and coarsely chopped**
- 2 **bay leaves**
- 1 **teaspoon kosher or sea salt**
- 4 **cups low-sodium chicken or vegetable broth**
- 1 **22-ounce jar vacuum-packed roasted chestnuts (see "Note," above)**
- ¼ **cup heavy cream**

1. In a 4- to 5-quart heavy-bottomed pot over medium heat, cook bacon until very crispy. Remove bacon from pan, reserving the grease; then crumble bacon and set aside.
2. Drain off all but 3 tablespoons bacon drippings from the pot; then add olive oil, onion, celery, and carrots, and cook, stirring often, until onion is golden brown, 12 to 15 minutes. Add apple, bay leaves, and salt, and cook for 3 minutes; then add broth, scraping the bottom of the pot with a wooden spoon to pick up browned bits. Add chestnuts and cook until very tender, about 15 minutes.
3. Remove the bay leaves; then purée soup in batches in a blender. Return the puréed soup to the pot. Stir in the cream and check seasoning; add more, if you like. Serve warm, sprinkled with reserved bacon.

REAL CREAM OF MUSHROOM SOUP
(recipe on opposite page)

REAL CREAM OF MUSHROOM SOUP

Here's the soup that inspired the Campbell's classic. Cream of mushroom soup was wildly popular in the early 20th century, and if you try your hand at making it from scratch, you'll see that the real stuff has a freshness that could never come from a can.

TOTAL TIME: 50 MINUTES • **HANDS-ON TIME:** 35 MINUTES • **YIELD:** 4 TO 6 SERVINGS

6	tablespoons salted butter, divided
1	pound sliced fresh button mushrooms
1	small onion, minced
1	teaspoon kosher or sea salt, plus more to taste
¼	teaspoon freshly ground black pepper
3	tablespoons all-purpose flour
1	cup reduced-sodium chicken broth
2	cups whole milk or half-and-half
1½	cups sour cream, at room temperature

1. Melt 3 tablespoons butter in a 4- to 5-quart heavy-bottomed pot over medium-high heat. Add mushrooms, onion, salt, and pepper, and cook, stirring often, until golden brown, about 15 minutes. Transfer to a bowl and set aside.

2. Reduce heat to medium and melt remaining 3 tablespoons butter. Add flour and cook, stirring, until glossy, about 3 minutes. Slowly drizzle in chicken broth and milk (or half-and-half), whisking as you do. Increase heat to a simmer and cook until the mixture thickens, whisking often, about 5 minutes.

3. Reduce heat to medium-low, stir in the reserved mushroom mixture, and cook 10 minutes, stirring occasionally. Remove from heat and add the sour cream. Serve hot.

CORN CHOWDER

Fresh summer corn is best served in the simplest ways. Too many other ingredients and you'll miss the delicate caramel and grain flavors that underlie the initial burst of sweetness. This recipe uses both the corn kernels and the milk scraped from the cob for maximum flavor.

TOTAL TIME: 40 MINUTES • HANDS-ON TIME: 30 MINUTES • YIELD: 4 TO 6 SERVINGS

6 ears fresh corn

3 cups whole milk

2 tablespoons salted butter

1 small onion, diced

2½ teaspoons kosher or sea salt

½ teaspoon freshly ground black pepper

1 tablespoon all-purpose flour

Garnish: chopped fresh parsley

1. Shuck the corn and score each row of kernels with a sharp knife. Use the dull side of the knife to scrape the pulp and corn milk from the cobs into a wide bowl. Pour the whole milk into a small saucepan over medium heat and bring to a low simmer.

2. Melt the butter in a 4- to 5-quart heavy-bottomed pot over medium heat. Add the onion, salt, and pepper, and cook, stirring often, until translucent, about 6 minutes. Stir in flour and corn and cook for 2 minutes. Add whole milk and bring to a simmer; the mixture will thicken. Serve hot, garnished with parsley.

WATERCRESS SOUP

The peppery flavor of watercress is complemented by the warming qualities of fresh ginger root. It brings a subtle Asian accent to this substantial soup, which can stand as supper when accompanied by chunks of bread.

TOTAL TIME: 55 MINUTES • HANDS-ON TIME: 45 MINUTES • YIELD: 8 MAIN-COURSE SERVINGS

3 tablespoons olive oil

6 large leeks, washed thoroughly and thinly sliced, white and pale-green parts only

3 medium-size yellow onions, thinly sliced

3 cloves garlic, minced

1 2-inch knob of fresh ginger root, peeled and finely chopped

6 large potatoes, peeled and cut into 1-inch cubes

6–7 cups reduced-sodium chicken broth

3 bunches watercress, stems removed and coarsely chopped

½ cup whole milk

Kosher or sea salt and freshly ground black pepper, to taste

Pinch nutmeg

Garnish: sour cream or plain Greek-style yogurt

(recipe continues on next page)

1. In a 4- to 5-quart heavy-bottomed pot, warm the olive oil over medium heat. Add the leeks and cook, stirring, until they soften, about 5 minutes. Stir in the onions and cook 3 more minutes. Add the garlic and ginger root and cook until all the vegetables are soft, 5 to 7 minutes longer.

2. Stir the potatoes into the leek/onion mixture; then add 6 cups of the broth. Raise heat to high and bring to a boil. Lower heat to medium-low and simmer, covered, until potatoes are tender, about 10 minutes. Add the watercress to the pot and simmer until the leaves are wilted, about 5 minutes.

3. Purée in a food processor in batches. Return purée to the soup pot; add the milk, salt, pepper, and nutmeg, and warm over medium-low heat for a few minutes. If the soup is too thick for your taste, add more broth. Serve garnished with a dollop of sour cream or yogurt.

LENTIL SOUP WITH HAM

This soup needs a bit of simmering time, which makes it a perfect choice for Sunday lunch or dinner. For a vegetarian option, eliminate the ham bone and the turmeric and add 1 to 2 teaspoons smoked paprika.

TOTAL TIME: 1 HOUR 45 MINUTES • **HANDS-ON TIME:** 30 MINUTES • **YIELD:** 8 TO 10 SERVINGS

2 **cups dry brown lentils**
2½ **quarts cold water**
1 **smoked ham bone (about 1 pound)**
3 **tablespoons salted butter**
2 **small onions, peeled and chopped**
4 **medium-size carrots, peeled and chopped**
3 **stalks celery, chopped**
2 **teaspoons ground turmeric**
1 **teaspoon cumin powder**
½ **teaspoon chili powder**
1½ **teaspoons kosher or sea salt, plus more to taste**
½ **teaspoon freshly ground black pepper, plus more to taste**
Garnish: 3 tablespoons chopped fresh parsley

1. Combine lentils and water in a 5- to 6-quart heavy-bottomed pot. Add the ham bone, partially cover the pot, and simmer, stirring occasionally, until lentils are just barely tender, 45 minutes to 1 hour. Add more liquid as necessary.

2. As lentils finish cooking, melt butter in a large skillet over medium heat. Add onions, carrots, and celery, and cook until onions are translucent, about 6 minutes. Add turmeric, cumin, chili powder, salt, and pepper, and cook, stirring, for 2 more minutes.

3. Add the vegetable mixture to the lentils in the pot. Simmer, partially covered, until lentils are fully cooked, about 30 minutes longer. Remove the ham bone and set aside to cool. Cut the meat from the ham bone, chop, and add to the soup. Check seasoning and add more salt and pepper to taste. Garnish with parsley.

ASPARAGUS VINAIGRETTE

Serving poached vegetables in vinaigrette sauce is one of the French techniques that Julia Child popularized and America embraced. It has become less popular in our current era of grilled vegetables and high-protein salads. But sweet spring asparagus is particularly well suited to a nice soak in a shallot-scented dressing.

TOTAL TIME: 1 HOUR 5 MINUTES · **HANDS-ON TIME:** 20 MINUTES · **YIELD:** 4 TO 6 SERVINGS

NOTE: *Peeling the asparagus makes it more tender and refined, but it's not essential to the success of the dish.*

- 1 **pound asparagus, ends trimmed and peeled (see "Note," above)**
- 1½ **teaspoons kosher or sea salt, plus more to taste**
- ½ **teaspoon freshly ground black pepper**
- 3 **tablespoons freshly squeezed lemon juice**
- ½ **teaspoon mustard powder**
- ¼ **cup extra-virgin olive oil**
- 1 **shallot, minced**
- 2 **teaspoons minced fresh chervil or tarragon or 1 teaspoon dried chervil or tarragon**

1. Fill a 3- to 4-quart saucepan with about 1½ inches of water and set a steamer basket in the bottom. Add asparagus, cover, and set over high heat. Steam until crisp-tender, 5 to 10 minutes, depending on the thickness of the stalks. Immediately submerge the stalks in cold water. When cool, drain and transfer to absorbent paper. Pat the stalks dry and arrange them in a large serving dish. Sprinkle with salt and pepper.

2. In a small mixing bowl, whisk together the lemon juice and mustard until the mustard is dissolved. Whisk in the olive oil. Stir in the shallot and chervil (or tarragon). Pour the mixture over the asparagus and turn to coat the stalks. Cover the dish with plastic wrap.

3. Refrigerate until thoroughly chilled, about 45 minutes, turning the asparagus occasionally. To serve, spoon some of the dressing over the top of the spears.

ASPARAGUS VINAIGRETTE
(recipe on opposite page)

CHICKEN WALDORF SALAD

This is a modern interpretation of the classic Waldorf salad—a creation of Oscar Tschirky, the first maître d' hôtel of the Waldorf Astoria in New York. The original Waldorf salad was just apples and celery in mayonnaise. Over time, raisins and walnuts were added. But we've never been fans of fruit in mayonnaise or raisins in salads. So we replaced the raisins with red grapes and tossed them with apples and lettuce in a simple lemon vinaigrette. Then we mixed chicken, celery, and lots of toasted walnuts in a creamy dressing of Greek yogurt with mayo, lemon juice, tarragon, and onion. It's like a chicken salad mixed with a green salad combined with a fruit salad. And all those parts come together in a fresher, more flavorful whole.

TOTAL TIME: 40 MINUTES • **HANDS-ON TIME:** 40 MINUTES • **YIELD:** 4 SERVINGS AS A LUNCH ENTRÉE, 6 AS A SIDE DISH

NOTE: *A 1½-pound rotisserie chicken will give you enough meat for this salad. You may substitute fresh chives, chervil, or mint for the tarragon.*

FOR THE DRESSINGS:

- 1 tablespoon plus 3 tablespoons fresh lemon juice
- 1 tablespoon olive oil
- ½ teaspoon kosher or sea salt, divided
- ⅓ cup reduced-fat Greek-style yogurt
- 2 tablespoons mayonnaise
- 1 tablespoon minced fresh tarragon (see "Note," above)
- 1 teaspoon honey
- ½ teaspoon freshly grated lemon zest
- ¼ teaspoon freshly ground black pepper
- 2 tablespoons minced sweet onion, such as Walla Walla or Vidalia

FOR THE SALAD:

- ⅔ cup chopped walnuts
- ½ pound chicken breast and/or thigh meat (see "Note," above)
- 1½ large celery stalks, sliced crosswise very thinly
- 6 ounces butter lettuce (also called Boston or Bibb)
- 1 cup halved seedless red grapes
- 1 medium-size apple (Cortland, Gala, Ginger Gold, or Fuji are great for salads because they don't brown quickly), cored and cut into thin wedges

1. First, make the dressings: In a small bowl, whisk together 1 tablespoon lemon juice with the olive oil and ¼ teaspoon salt. Set aside. In another small bowl, stir together the remaining 3 tablespoons lemon juice, yogurt, mayonnaise, tarragon, honey, lemon zest, remaining ¼ teaspoon salt, and pepper. Stir in onion. Set aside while you prepare the salad.

2. Toast walnuts in a large dry skillet over medium-low heat, stirring occasionally, until brown and fragrant, about 10 minutes. Pour into a medium-size bowl, and let cool as you prepare the chicken: Remove any skin and tear the chicken into 2- or 3-inch strips. Add to the bowl with the walnuts. Add the celery and the yogurt dressing, and stir to cover ingredients evenly.

3. In your serving bowl, toss the lettuce, grapes, and apple wedges with the lemon/oil dressing. Spoon the chicken mixture over all. Use your hands to lightly fluff the leaves and grapes, just to make it look pretty. Serve on chilled salad plates.

CHICKEN WALDORF SALAD
(recipe on opposite page)

MOM'S CARAWAY COLESLAW

This recipe first ran in the May 2000 issue of Yankee, a submission from a reader named Mary Connelly Benway, whose mother had made it for her brood of 10 children. "All of us are grown now, some in middle age," she writes. "My mother has always been, and still is, the best cook I know. Whether it was a summer lunch at a wooded lakeside, a visit to the Rhode Island seashore, or a family car trip to the White Mountains, our tailgate picnics were always abundant and delectable . . . By preparing these favorite dishes in my own kitchen for more than 20 years, I have managed to convince my husband that I am a pretty good cook—a tribute to her." We love the way this classic coleslaw manages to be sweet, savory, tangy, and creamy all in a single bite.

TOTAL TIME: 30 MINUTES • **HANDS-ON TIME:** 30 MINUTES • **YIELD:** 6 TO 8 SERVINGS

3½ cups finely shredded green or purple cabbage
2 large carrots, peeled and grated
1 green bell pepper, finely chopped
½ cup mayonnaise
1 small white or sweet onion, grated
2 tablespoons fresh lemon juice
1 tablespoon white or cider vinegar
1 tablespoon granulated sugar
1 teaspoon whole caraway seeds
½ teaspoon mustard powder
  Kosher or sea salt and freshly ground black pepper,
    to taste

1. In a large bowl, toss together cabbage, carrots, and bell pepper. In a small bowl, whisk together remaining ingredients. Pour dressing over vegetables and toss well. Let sit at least 20 minutes before serving.

HARVARD BEETS

According to John Mariani's Encyclopedia of American Food and Drink, *the name of this dish—which became very popular around the turn of the 20th century—"probably comes from the deep crimson color of cooked beets, similar to the color of the Harvard football team's jersey." However, Mariani notes an alternative theory, as put forth in the* New York Times *in 1982, that "the dish was conceived at a seventeenth-century English tavern called Harwood's, whose customers included a Russian émigré who, in 1846, opened up a restaurant in Boston under the same name. But the émigré kept pronouncing his establishment's name more like 'Harvard,' so the dish he brought from England is known as 'Harvard beets.'" To be honest, the football-jersey explanation sounds more likely to us, but as with much of food history, we may never know the true answer.*

TOTAL TIME: 1½ HOURS • **HANDS-ON TIME:** 25 MINUTES • **YIELD:** 6 SERVINGS

3 medium-size beets (about 2 pounds), ideally a mix of red, yellow, and Chioggia colors
½ cup granulated sugar
½ teaspoon kosher or sea salt
½ cup white vinegar
1 tablespoon cornstarch
2 whole cloves
2 tablespoons unsalted butter

1. Preheat the oven to 375° and put a rack in the middle of the oven. Wash and trim the beets, leaving an inch of leaf stems and all the root.
2. Wrap the beets tightly in aluminum foil and put in the oven. Roast until fork-tender, 45 minutes to 1 hour. When cool enough to handle, peel using a small knife or your fingers; then slice into ¼-inch-thick rounds.
3. In a double boiler over medium heat, whisk together sugar, salt, vinegar, cornstarch, and cloves. Cook, stirring gently, until the mixture is clear.
4. Add sliced beets; then reduce heat and simmer for 20 minutes.
5. Remove cloves and add butter just before serving.

**SQUASH GRATIN
WITH GARLIC & ROSEMARY**
(recipe on page 55)

Vegetable Entrées and Sides

Every cook should make a cheese soufflé at least once in his or her life. But if that sounds too ambitious (for now), how about trying "woodchuck," an old Yankee cheese-and-corn sauce made to be served on toast or dipped with crusty bread? Or an easy pumpkin custard that makes a delectable Thanksgiving side dish? And when summer rolls around, don't forget our corn pudding, broiled tomatoes, and zucchini pancakes.

BROILED TOMATOES

We love a good heirloom-tomato salad as much as anyone, but it's nice to remember the magic that a few breadcrumbs and some grated cheese can bring to these sweet summer fruits.

TOTAL TIME: 15 MINUTES • HANDS-ON TIME: 10 MINUTES • YIELD: 4 TO 6 SERVINGS

6   ripe plum tomatoes, halved lengthwise
¼   cup plain breadcrumbs
3   tablespoons salted butter, softened
3   tablespoons freshly grated Parmesan cheese
2   teaspoons minced fresh thyme leaves
1   teaspoon kosher or sea salt
½   teaspoon freshly ground black pepper

1. Preheat the broiler. Line a rimmed sheet pan with aluminum foil, shiny side up, and set an oven rack to the top position. Arrange tomato halves in the pan.
2. In a small bowl, stir together the remaining ingredients. Sprinkle the mixture over the tomatoes; then transfer to the top shelf of the oven and broil until nicely browned, 3 to 5 minutes.

ZUCCHINI PANCAKES

These pancakes are a great way to serve summer's most abundant vegetable. They go well with most meats and can even be served as a main course. For added color, replace ½ cup of the zucchini with grated carrot. Serve pancakes plain, or top with Greek yogurt or sour cream, plus smoked salmon or prosciutto.

TOTAL TIME: 40 MINUTES • HANDS-ON TIME: 20 MINUTES • YIELD: 12 PANCAKES OR 4 SERVINGS

2   cups grated unpeeled zucchini squash
1   teaspoon kosher or sea salt
¾   cup all-purpose flour
2   teaspoons baking powder
½   cup grated cheddar or Colby cheese
1   tablespoon thinly sliced scallions (green onions)
     or 2 tablespoons finely chopped fresh chives
2   large eggs, lightly beaten
2   tablespoons salted butter, melted
1   tablespoon cold salted butter, divided

1. Toss zucchini with the salt in a colander and let stand for 10 minutes. Squeeze out any remaining liquid.
2. In a medium-size mixing bowl, whisk together the flour and baking powder. Stir in the cheese and scallions; then add eggs, melted butter, and zucchini and mix until well combined.
3. Melt 1 teaspoon of the cold butter in a large skillet over medium heat. Spoon batter by the tablespoon into the pan, being careful not to overcrowd. Press down lightly with a spatula to flatten. Brown pancakes lightly on each side, about 4 minutes per side; then transfer to a baking sheet and keep warm in a 200° oven until serving. Repeat with remaining batter and butter.

**BROILED TOMATOES,
ZUCCHINI PANCAKES**
(recipes on opposite page)

ZUCCHINI CUTLETS

We found this recipe in Yankee's *archives, listed as a favorite of Mrs. Connie deAngelo of Boston, "one of the few women regulars on Blackstone Street, Haymarket, Boston." We can only assume she was one of the regular vendors, not shoppers, since women shopped Boston's famous discount vegetable market in droves (and still do). In the original recipe, Connie recommends serving the cutlets with a sprinkle of parsley or with tomato sauce.*

TOTAL TIME: 30 MINUTES · **HANDS-ON TIME:** 30 MINUTES · **YIELD:** 6 SERVINGS

3 **large zucchini squash**

2 **large eggs**

½ **teaspoon kosher or sea salt, plus more to taste**

¼ **teaspoon freshly ground black pepper**

2 **rounded tablespoons grated Romano cheese**

1 **cup seasoned breadcrumbs**

6 **tablespoons olive oil, divided**

1. Trim the ends from the zucchini and cut lengthwise into strips about 1 inch wide, 4 inches long, and ½ inch thick. In a small bowl, beat the eggs with ½ teaspoon salt and the pepper. In a shallow bowl, stir together the cheese and breadcrumbs. Dip the slices of zucchini in the egg; then drag through the breadcrumb/cheese mixture to coat.

2. Heat 3 tablespoons of the olive oil in a large (12- to 14-inch) skillet over medium heat. Add half the zucchini slices, and brown on both sides, 3 to 4 minutes per side. Turn gently to avoid breaking the slices. Remove to a heated platter, wipe the pan, and repeat with the remaining oil and zucchini. Sprinkle lightly with additional salt, to taste.

CORN PUDDING

When the first European settlers began experimenting with the "Indian" corn that sustained them, they found that this Native American grain was a better match for British-style puddings than breads. Vegetable puddings made with eggs and milk or cream were documented in English cookery books in the 17th century, so it wasn't a big leap for New Englanders to begin cooking corn in custard. The dish remains as simple and delicious today.

TOTAL TIME: 1 HOUR 30 MINUTES • **HANDS-ON TIME:** 30 MINUTES • **YIELD:** 6 SERVINGS

NOTE: *Fresh corn kernels right off the cob are always best, but frozen corn will do in a pinch.*

- **3 tablespoons salted butter, plus more for dish**
- **2 cups whole corn kernels (see "Note," above)**
- **2 tablespoons all-purpose flour**
- **2 tablespoons granulated sugar**
- **1 teaspoon table salt**
- **3 large eggs**
- **1 3/4 cups milk**

1. Preheat the oven to 325° and grease a 1½-quart casserole dish.
2. Put 3 tablespoons butter, plus corn, flour, sugar, and salt, into a blender or food processor and pulse until combined. Add eggs, one at a time, mixing after each addition. Add milk and blend. Pour into the prepared dish and bake until set, about 1 hour, stirring once after 20 minutes.

**CORN PUDDING,
NEW ENGLAND SUCCOTASH**
(recipes on page 45 and opposite)

NEW ENGLAND SUCCOTASH

A combination of cranberry beans and corn kernels, succotash was one of the first foods that the Native Americans of coastal New England shared with the Plymouth settlers. Rich in nutrients and inexpensive to make, it was especially popular during the Depression and World War II.

TOTAL TIME: 45 MINUTES · HANDS-ON TIME: 20 MINUTES · YIELD: 6 TO 8 SERVINGS

NOTE: *Cranberry beans are closest to the type of bean that would have originally been used in this dish, but fresh or frozen lima beans are a popular substitute.*

- **6 ears fresh corn**
- **4 tablespoons unsalted butter, divided**
- **3 pounds fresh (not dried) cranberry beans or fresh or frozen lima beans, shelled (see "Note," above)**
- **⅛ pound salt pork, cut into 4 pieces (optional)**
- **½ small onion, minced**
- **2 teaspoons granulated sugar**
  Kosher or sea salt and freshly ground black pepper, to taste
- **¼ cup heavy cream (optional)**

1. Use a sharp knife to cut the kernels from the cobs and set aside.
2. In a large saucepan over medium heat, melt 1 tablespoon butter. Add the beans, salt pork (if using), and onion. Cook, stirring often, until the beans are tender and the onion is golden, about 10 minutes.
3. Stir in the corn and add enough water to cover by ½ inch. Add the sugar and remaining 3 tablespoons butter. Bring to a gentle bubble and cook, uncovered, for 10 minutes.
4. Remove the salt pork and season with salt and pepper to taste. Add cream, if you like. Serve hot.

CHEESE WOODCHUCK

The origins of this recipe are fodder for a good debate, best argued over a plate of this corn-and-cheese sauce on crusty toasted bread. Theory #1: In a 1966 issue of Yankee, *reader Mildred B. Larrabee shared this recipe, along with the story of an ill-fated ship from Amsterdam that foundered in a storm off the coast of Maine, in December 1710. On board: hundreds of wheels of wax-coated cheese, many of which floated safely to shore on Peaks Island (the crew were not so lucky). "The women [on the island] were hard-taxed to find ways in which to utilize it in such ingenious recipes as to avoid the exclamation: 'Oh, not cheese again!'" Larrabee's kin had deep roots on Peaks Island, and she theorized that this old family recipe might have come from that period. Theory #2: Another "woodchuck" dish, on record from the 1930s, uses canned tomatoes or tomato soup in a flour-thickened sauce with melted cheese. Both are essentially variations on Welsh rarebit. So is this a pre-Revolutionary treat or a 20th-century invention? It's delicious either way.*

TOTAL TIME: 30 MINUTES • **HANDS-ON TIME:** 30 MINUTES • **YIELD:** 3 SERVINGS AS A MAIN COURSE, 6 AS A SNACK

- **2 tablespoons salted butter**
- **1 small onion, minced**
- **1 teaspoon kosher or sea salt**
- **½ cup milk**
- **½ pound sharp cheese (such as aged Gouda or cheddar), grated**
- **2 large egg yolks, beaten**
- **2 cups fresh corn, scraped from about 3 cobs**
- **2 teaspoons minced fresh parsley or savory**
- **6 slices toasted sourdough or other crusty bread**
  Garnish: minced parsley, savory, or chives

1. Melt butter in a medium-size skillet over medium heat. Add onion and salt and cook until translucent, about 6 minutes. Reduce heat to medium-low, add milk, and stir until slightly thickened, about 5 minutes. Reduce heat to the lowest setting and sprinkle in cheese, stirring continuously.

2. When fully melted, spoon ¼ cup of the mixture into a small bowl with the egg yolks, whisking as you do (see p. 181, top). Whisk in an additional ¼ cup of the mixture; then pour back into the pot. Stir until thickened. Add corn and parsley. Serve hot over toast and garnished with fresh herbs.

COLCANNON

This traditional Irish dish is composed of shredded cabbage or kale and buttery mashed potatoes blended with thinly sliced green onions and chopped fresh parsley. There's even a song about it, done in traditional Irish folk style:

> *Did you ever eat Colcannon, made from lovely pickled cream,*
> *With the greens and scallions mingled like a picture in a dream?*
> *Did you ever make a hole on top to hold the melting flake*
> *Of the creamy, flavored butter that your mother used to make?*
> *Yes you did, so you did, so did he and so did I,*
> *And the more I think about it, sure the nearer I'm to cry.*
> *Oh, wasn't it the happy days when troubles we had not,*
> *And our mothers made Colcannon in the little skillet pot.*

TOTAL TIME: 1 HOUR • **HANDS-ON TIME:** 1 HOUR • **YIELD:** 6 SERVINGS

- **4** large russet potatoes, peeled and cut into quarters
- ⅓ cup light or heavy cream
- **8** tablespoons salted butter, divided
- **1** small head green cabbage, shredded, or about 2 pounds fresh kale, shredded
- **8** scallions (green onions), white and green portions, thinly sliced
- ½ cup water
-   Kosher or sea salt, plus more for cooking potatoes
-   Freshly ground black pepper, to taste
- **2** tablespoons chopped fresh parsley

1. Drop the potatoes into a large pot of boiling, salted water. Reduce heat to low and cook, uncovered, at a gentle bubble until tender when pierced, 20 to 30 minutes. Drain; then return potatoes to the pot. Immediately break up the potatoes with a fork or potato masher to release the steam. Add the cream and 4 tablespoons of the butter and beat with a wooden spoon until smooth.

2. Melt the remaining 4 tablespoons of butter in a large skillet and add the shredded cabbage or kale. Stir over medium heat until just wilted, 5 to 7 minutes. Add the scallions and water. Continue stirring until the cabbage is very tender and the liquid evaporates, 7 to 10 minutes more. Season with salt and pepper to taste.

3. Add the cabbage mixture and parsley to the potatoes in the pot. Return the pot to medium heat and cook, stirring, until the potatoes are heated through. Transfer to a serving bowl and serve piping hot.

CHEESE SOUFFLÉ

We have Julia Child to thank for doing the most to popularize this beautiful and useful dish. Cheese soufflé always can be counted on to impress your guests, and it's easy to make. This recipe is for a 6-cup soufflé mold and serves three amply. If it's to be the main dish for four or five people, make 1½ times the recipe (6 egg yolks and 7 or 8 whites) and use an 8-cup mold. For 6 servings, double the recipe and use two 6-cup molds.

TOTAL TIME: 1 HOUR • **HANDS-ON TIME:** 20 MINUTES • **YIELD:** 3 SERVINGS

2½ **tablespoons unsalted butter, plus more for dish**
2 **tablespoons freshly grated Parmesan or Romano cheese**
3 **tablespoons all-purpose flour**
1 **cup milk**
½ **teaspoon table salt**
¼ **teaspoon mustard powder**
⅛ **teaspoon cayenne pepper**
1 **cup (about 5 ounces) shredded sharp cheddar cheese**
4 **large egg yolks, at room temperature**
5 **large egg whites, at room temperature**

1. Preheat the oven to 400° and set a rack to the middle position. Butter a straight-sided soufflé dish well, and shake the grated cheese around it to coat.

2. In a 3- to 4-quart saucepan, melt 2½ tablespoons butter over medium heat; then stir in flour. Reduce heat to low and gradually drizzle in milk, whisking continuously. Stir in salt, mustard, and cayenne; then add cheese and mix well. (The sauce will be thick.) Transfer to a large bowl and cool for 5 minutes. Stir yolks one by one into the sauce and set aside.

3. In a large, very clean mixing bowl, beat the egg whites until they form firm peaks. Stir a generous dollop of beaten whites into the sauce to lighten it; then very quickly and lightly fold in the rest of the whites. Spoon mixture into the prepared dish and place on the rack in the center of the oven. Immediately reduce heat to 375°.

4. In 25 to 30 minutes, the soufflé should be well puffed but still creamy in the center. Let it cook 5 minutes longer and take it to the table, where you've already assembled your guests and the other elements of the meal.

SPINACH CRÊPES

TOTAL TIME: 1 HOUR • **HANDS-ON TIME:** 40 MINUTES • **YIELD:** 10 CRÊPES

FOR THE BATTER:

- 1 cup milk
- 2 large eggs
- 1 cup all-purpose flour
- ¼ cup water
- 3 tablespoons salted butter, melted
- ½ teaspoon table salt

FOR THE FILLING:

- 3 tablespoons salted butter
- 10 ounces sliced button mushrooms
- 2 tablespoons minced shallots
- 1½ tablespoons all-purpose flour
- 1 cup chicken or vegetable broth
- 10 ounces fresh baby spinach
- 2 ounces (⅛ pound) Gruyère or cheddar cheese, grated
  Kosher or sea salt and freshly ground black pepper, to taste
- ¼ cup grated Parmesan cheese

1. Put the batter ingredients into a blender and mix until smooth. Let stand at least 30 minutes (or chill for up to 8 hours).

2. Make the filling: In a skillet over medium-high heat, melt butter and sauté mushrooms until golden brown, 8 to 10 minutes. Reduce heat to medium, add shallots, and cook 1 minute. Sprinkle flour evenly over vegetables and stir until coated. Add broth, stirring mixture until thickened. Add spinach and cook, stirring, until wilted, about 2 minutes. Remove from heat and stir in cheese. Season with salt and pepper.

3. Make the crêpes: Mist a crêpe pan with no-stick spray; warm over medium heat. For each crêpe, pour in ¼ cup batter, instantly swirling around pan to spread evenly to the edges in a thin film. Cook quickly until golden brown, 1 to 2 minutes; then turn and brown other side, about 1 more minute. Pile cooked crêpes on top of one another, keeping warm under an inverted plate or pot lid (if you must keep them warm a while, store in a low oven). Divide filling among crêpes; then fold around filling. Sprinkle with cheese.

PUMPKIN CUSTARD

With all its sweetness and warm spice, and a texture somewhere between a custard and a soufflé, this dish is a bit like eating dessert for dinner. Rose Traverso, grandmother of Yankee *senior lifestyle editor Amy Traverso, served it every year at Thanksgiving.*

TOTAL TIME: 1 HOUR 10 MINUTES • **HANDS-ON TIME:** 15 MINUTES • **YIELD:** 6 SERVINGS

Butter for dish
3 **large eggs**
⅓ **cup granulated sugar**
1¼ **cups canned pumpkin purée**
½ **cup evaporated milk**
1 **tablespoon all-purpose flour**
1 **teaspoon ground cinnamon**
1 **teaspoon kosher or sea salt**
½ **teaspoon ground ginger**
¼ **teaspoon ground cloves**
¼ **teaspoon ground allspice**

1. Preheat the oven to 425° and set a rack to the middle position. Butter a 1½-quart soufflé dish. Fill a kettle with about 4 cups water and bring to a simmer.
2. Meanwhile, in a large bowl, using a standing or hand-held mixer, beat the eggs and sugar at medium-high speed for 2 minutes, until thick and pale yellow. Gently fold in the remaining ingredients.
3. Pour the custard into the prepared dish and set in a baking pan. Transfer both to the oven; then fill the baking pan with enough of the simmering water to come halfway up the sides of the dish. Bake for 10 minutes. Reduce the heat to 350° and bake until the center of the custard barely jiggles when shaken, 30 to 45 more minutes. Let sit for 10 minutes; then serve warm or at room temperature.

GLAZED ORANGE-SCENTED PARSNIPS

For a hardy root vegetable, parsnips have a remarkably tropical flavor, one that goes so beautifully with orange marmalade.

TOTAL TIME: 35 MINUTES • **HANDS-ON TIME:** 15 MINUTES • **YIELD:** 4 SERVINGS

NOTE: *If your parsnips are especially thick (more than 1 inch across), quarter them lengthwise.*

- **1 pound parsnips, peeled and halved lengthwise (see "Note," above)**
- **6 tablespoons salted butter, divided**
- **1 cup water**
- **1 teaspoon kosher or sea salt**
- **¼ teaspoon freshly ground black pepper**
- **¼ teaspoon freshly grated nutmeg**
- **¼ cup orange marmalade**
- **Juice of 1 lemon**

1. Cut the parsnips into 1-inch lengths.
2. Melt 4 tablespoons of the butter in a large skillet over medium heat. Add the parsnips and toss to coat. Pour in the water and cover the pan. Simmer until parsnips are tender when pierced, 15 to 20 minutes.
3. Sprinkle parsnips with salt, pepper, and nutmeg. Add the remaining 2 tablespoons of butter, the marmalade, and lemon juice. Increase the heat and stir continuously until the liquid evaporates and a syrupy glaze is left. Toss to coat all the nuggets evenly and transfer to a vegetable dish. Serve warm.

SQUASH GRATIN WITH GARLIC & ROSEMARY

Mac-and-cheese—essentially a gratin made with pasta—is one of America's favorite foods. So why not sweet butternut squash in a creamy cheese sauce with a toasted breadcrumb topping? It's festive enough for the Thanksgiving table.

TOTAL TIME: 1 HOUR 25 MINUTES • **HANDS-ON TIME:** 55 MINUTES • **YIELD:** 6 SERVINGS

2	tablespoons heavy cream
3	tablespoons reduced-sodium chicken or vegetable broth
1	medium-size butternut squash, peeled, seeded, and cut into ¼-inch-thick crescents and half-moons
4	ounces (¼ pound) Gruyère cheese, grated
1¼	teaspoons kosher or sea salt, divided
¾	teaspoon freshly ground black pepper, divided
4	tablespoons salted butter, divided
1	large yellow onion, diced
2	teaspoons minced fresh rosemary
1½	ounces crusty white bread, torn into small pieces
2	cloves garlic, minced
½	teaspoon freshly grated nutmeg

1. Preheat the oven to 350° and set an oven rack to the middle position. In a large bowl, whisk together cream and broth; then add squash, cheese, 1 teaspoon salt, and ½ teaspoon pepper. Toss well. Pour into a large gratin or baking dish, cover with foil, and bake until squash is tender, 35 to 45 minutes, turning the dish and removing the foil halfway through. Remove from the oven and set aside. Leave the oven on.

2. Meanwhile, melt 3 tablespoons butter in a skillet over medium-high heat. Add diced onion, and cook, stirring occasionally, until it begins to brown, about 10 minutes. Add rosemary, remaining ¼ teaspoon salt, and ¼ teaspoon pepper; cook until fragrant, about 1 minute. Spread evenly over squash. Turn the broiler to high.

3. In a food processor, pulse bread with remaining 1 tablespoon butter, garlic, and nutmeg to create coarse breadcrumbs. Sprinkle over squash. Broil, uncovered, until topping is golden brown, 5 to 7 minutes. Let rest at least 20 minutes before serving.

PORTUGUESE FISHERMAN'S STEW
(recipe on page 77)

Meat and Seafood Entrées

Rediscover the joy of childhood favorites such as real Swedish meatballs and turkey Tetrazzini, or find ultimate comfort in our chicken and dumplings or chicken pot pies with cheddar-biscuit crusts. Then celebrate New England's coastal cuisine with an old-fashioned lobster pie— or the most delicious red clam sauce you'll ever taste.

ALL-STAR CHICKEN & DUMPLINGS
(recipe on opposite page)

ALL-STAR CHICKEN & DUMPLINGS

The word dumpling *goes back to 17th-century England, but the practice of cooking little pieces of dough in soup or stew goes back much further, in both Europe and Asia. Chicken and dumplings like these, in which lightly leavened dough is cooked in chicken stew, have their roots in Pennsylvania German and Acadian cooking. This dish, which we've adapted from our friends at* The Old Farmer's Almanac, *is a wonderfully efficient way to use a chicken. The whole bird goes into the pot to make the broth, and then the meat is added back in at the end with some aromatics and the dumplings.*

To make this dish easier, we made the dumplings by simply dropping them into the broth, rather than rolling them out and cutting them into strips. This is one of the most satisfying and comforting foods you can make, perfect for any rainy or snowy or otherwise sniffly day.

TOTAL TIME: 2 HOURS • **HANDS-ON TIME:** 1 HOUR • **YIELD:** 8 TO 10 SERVINGS

FOR THE SOUP:
- 1 **whole 4- to 5-pound chicken**
- 5 **bay leaves**
- 4 **tablespoons salted butter**
- 1½ **tablespoons table salt, plus more to taste**
- ½ **teaspoon freshly ground black pepper**
- 4 **large carrots, sliced into half-moons about ½ inch thick**
- 2 **large stalks celery, sliced crosswise about ¼ inch thick**
- 1 **large yellow onion, diced**
  Garnish: minced fresh parsley

FOR THE DUMPLINGS:
- 3 **cups all-purpose flour, plus more for work surface**
- 1½ **teaspoons baking powder**
- 1 **teaspoon table salt**
- ½ **cup vegetable oil**
- ¾ **cup water**
- 2 **small or medium-size eggs**

1. Wash the chicken and put into a large soup pot. Cover with 1 to 2 inches of water and add bay leaves, butter, salt, and pepper. Cover, set over high heat, and bring to a boil. Reduce heat to low, partially cover, and simmer gently until the chicken is cooked through, about 1 hour.

2. When the chicken is done, transfer it to a cutting board, leaving the broth and bay leaves in the pot. When the chicken is cool enough to handle, pull the meat from the bone in small pieces and set aside. (Discard the bones, skin, and other waste).

3. Meanwhile, make the dumplings: In a large bowl, whisk together the flour, baking powder, and salt. Add the oil and stir to coat the flour; then add the water and eggs. Stir just enough to combine.

4. Bring the broth back to a boil and add carrots, celery, and onion. Drop the dumpling dough into the boiling broth, a heaping tablespoon at a time, to form balls. Boil approximately 20 minutes, uncovered, stirring occasionally to prevent sticking, until the dumplings are done (they'll be slightly puffed) and the broth is a bit thicker. Return the chicken to the pot in the last 5 minutes of cooking. Remove bay leaves before serving. Serve hot, garnished with parsley.

CHICKEN POT PIES WITH CHEDDAR–SCALLION BISCUITS

It's hard to imagine a more comforting combination than savory chicken pot pie filling topped with cheesy biscuits. Butternut squash replaces the usual potatoes for a nice hit of color and sweetness.

TOTAL TIME: 1 HOUR 20 MINUTES · **HANDS-ON TIME:** 1 HOUR · **YIELD:** 6 TO 7 SERVINGS

NOTE: *Using precooked rotisserie chicken meat saves valuable prep time.*

MAKE-AHEAD TIP: *Prepare pies up to the point of baking; then wrap tightly in foil and freeze for up to 3 months. When ready to use, let them sit at room temperature for 15 minutes; then bake at 400° for 35 to 45 minutes.*

FOR THE FILLING:

- 3 cups reduced-sodium chicken broth
- 3 medium-size carrots, peeled and diced
- ½ small butternut squash, peeled, seeded, and diced
- 4 tablespoons salted butter
- 1 large celery rib, diced
- 1 medium-size yellow onion, diced
- 1 teaspoon kosher or sea salt
- 1 cup roughly chopped white button mushrooms
- 5 tablespoons all-purpose flour
- 1 cup milk
- ½ teaspoon freshly ground black pepper
- 2 tablespoons minced flat-leaf parsley
- 3 cups chopped cooked chicken, white and dark meat (see "Note," above)
- ⅓ cup sweet peas (frozen is fine)

FOR THE BISCUITS:

- 2 cups all-purpose flour, plus more for work surface
- 2 teaspoons baking powder
- ½ teaspoon baking soda
- ½ teaspoon table salt
- 5 tablespoons cold salted butter, cut into small cubes
- ⅔ cup grated sharp cheddar cheese
- 2 scallions (green onions), green parts only, thinly sliced
- 1 large egg
- ⅔ cup buttermilk
- Milk (for brushing biscuits)

1. First, make the filling: In a medium-size saucepan over high heat, bring chicken broth to a boil. Add carrots and squash. Reduce heat to medium-low and simmer until vegetables are tender, 5 to 7 minutes. Drain vegetables, reserving broth. Set aside.

2. Melt butter in a large skillet over medium heat. Add celery, onion, and salt; cook until golden, 10 to 12 minutes. Add mushrooms and cook until they release most of their liquid, 5 to 7 minutes. Add flour and cook, stirring, about 2 minutes. Add milk slowly, whisking as you do; then add reserved broth, whisking until smooth. Cook, stirring often, until sauce thickens, 8 to 10 minutes. Season with pepper. Add parsley, chicken, reserved vegetables, and peas. Divide filling evenly among 6 ramekins or other 8- to 10-ounce ovenproof bowls, leaving about a half-inch at the top for biscuits. If you have extra filling, put it in another ramekin.

3. Preheat the oven to 425°. Make the biscuits: In a large bowl, whisk flour with baking powder, baking soda, and salt. Working quickly so that the butter stays cold (see p. 181, bottom), use your fingers to smear the butter into the flour mixture until it resembles coarse meal, with plenty of lumps. Stir in cheddar and scallions. In a medium-size bowl, whisk together egg and buttermilk; add to flour mixture. Stir with a fork until a shaggy dough forms. Don't overmix.

(recipe continues on next page)

4. Divide dough into two balls. On a lightly floured counter, press dough out to a ½-inch thickness. Using a floured biscuit cutter or rim of a glass, cut out 2- to 3-inch rounds. Gather dough again as needed and press out again. Repeat with second dough ball.

5. Divide biscuits among ramekins, overlapping as necessary. Brush tops with milk, and set ramekins on a baking sheet lined with foil. Bake until crust is nicely browned and filling is bubbling, about 20 minutes.

CHICKEN CACCIATORE

Reader Fredericka Jones shared this recipe with us about 10 years ago. It arrived via Ellis Island with her father, Louis Janus Vici; he cut a dashing figure in World War I, serving in the Air Corps as a navigator, gunner, and bombardier. He was a great cook, too, if this recipe is any evidence.

TOTAL TIME: 1½ HOURS · **HANDS-ON TIME:** 45 MINUTES · **YIELD:** 6 SERVINGS

1	**3- to 4-pound chicken, cut into 8 parts**
2½	**teaspoons kosher or sea salt, divided**
½	**teaspoon freshly ground black pepper**
3	**tablespoons salted butter**
1	**tablespoon olive oil**
1	**medium-size onion, finely chopped**
½	**pound fresh button mushrooms, sliced**
2	**tablespoons all-purpose flour**
½	**cup dry white wine, such as Pinot Grigio**
2	**tablespoons cognac**
1	**cup reduced-sodium chicken broth**
3	**cups canned diced tomatoes, drained**
1–2	**cloves garlic, minced**
2	**tablespoons chopped fresh parsley**
2	**tablespoons chopped fresh basil**
½	**teaspoon dried oregano**

1. Rinse chicken; pat dry and season all over with 2 teaspoons salt and the pepper. In a 4- to 5-quart oven-safe pot over medium-high heat, melt butter with oil. Add chicken and brown on all sides, working in batches to avoid overcrowding. Remove and set aside.

2. Preheat the oven to 350°. Add onion, mushrooms, and remaining salt to pot. Cook, stirring often, until onion is translucent, about 6 minutes. Add flour and stir. Cook, stirring continuously, until glossy. Remove from heat; add wine, cognac, broth, tomatoes, and garlic. Return to heat and simmer 10 minutes. Return chicken to pot.

3. Cover and bake until chicken is cooked through, 45 to 55 minutes. Remove chicken and keep warm on a serving plate. Bring sauce to a boil in the pot on the stovetop; cook until volume is reduced to about 3 cups. Add herbs. Serve with crusty bread or over linguine or polenta.

**CHICKEN POT PIES
WITH CHEDDAR–SCALLION
BISCUITS**
(recipe on page 60)

CHICKEN À LA KING

This dish dates back more than 100 years—to sometime between 1800 and about 1910. As with many recipes, there are several stories of its origin: Was it an invention of a chef named William King, who worked at Philadelphia's Bellevue Hotel? A creation of chef George Greenwald, in honor of his boss, Mr. King, at New York's Brighton Beach Hotel? There are a few other theories, but no one knows the answer for certain.

In any case, the fundamentals of the dish include chicken in a cream sauce with mushrooms and peppers or pimentos, as well as some sherry or Madeira. Older versions of the recipe called for thickening the sauce with a combination of cream, egg yolks, and roux (a flour/butter mixture).

Over time the dish morphed into a heavy glop of chicken swimming in an overly flour-thickened sauce. Midcentury recipes even replaced the original sauce with cream of chicken soup; it became the stuff of cafeteria lines. But there's still a gem of deliciousness in this recipe, so we updated it with more vegetables, fresh herbs and shallots, less flour, and crème fraîche (or sour cream).

TOTAL TIME: 45 MINUTES • **HANDS-ON TIME:** 45 MINUTES • **YIELD:** 4 TO 5 SERVINGS

NOTE: *You can poach your own chicken for this recipe, but you can save time by using the meat from a rotisserie bird.*

- **3** teaspoons kosher or sea salt, divided
- **2** cups reduced-sodium chicken broth
- **3** tablespoons dry sherry
- **1** tablespoon salted butter
- **2** tablespoons olive oil
- **3** large shallots, minced
- **½** cup diced red bell pepper
- **¼** cup diced green bell pepper
- **2** cups sliced button mushrooms
- **1** pound egg noodles
- **3** tablespoons all-purpose flour
- **½** teaspoon paprika
- **2** sprigs fresh tarragon
- **2⅓** cups cooked shredded chicken (see "Note," above)
- **½** cup crème fraîche or sour cream
- **2** tablespoons minced fresh parsley
  Garnish: minced fresh parsley

1. Set a large pot of water seasoned with 2 teaspoons salt over high heat.
2. In a small saucepan over medium-high heat, bring broth and sherry to a simmer.
3. Meanwhile, melt butter in a 12-inch skillet over medium heat. Add oil, shallots, peppers, and remaining 1 teaspoon salt to the skillet and cook, stirring, until softened, about 5 minutes. Increase heat to medium-high, add mushrooms, and cook, stirring often, until lightly browned, about 7 minutes.
4. Meanwhile, when the water is boiling, add the egg noodles and cook according to package instructions. Drain and set aside.
5. Add flour and paprika to the skillet and cook, stirring, for 2 minutes. Add hot broth mixture in a thin stream, stirring as you go. The sauce should bubble and thicken. Add tarragon sprigs.
6. Reduce heat to low and add chicken, crème fraîche (or sour cream), and parsley. Cook 10 minutes; then serve over the egg noodles, with a sprinkling of additional parsley.

TURKEY TETRAZZINI

It may sound Italian, but tetrazzini is an American dish first invented in San Francisco in the early 1900s. It paid homage to soprano Luisa Tetrazzini, an Italian native who loved the city so much that she performed a free public concert there on Christmas Eve 1910, for a crowd estimated at more than 200,000. The dish caught on and soon became a favorite way to use up leftover turkey after Thanksgiving. We've modernized it with a little less cream and more vegetables.

TOTAL TIME: 1 HOUR • HANDS-ON TIME: 40 MINUTES • YIELD: 6 SERVINGS

NOTE: *If you're using chicken instead of turkey in this recipe, you can poach your own, but you can save time by using the meat from a rotisserie bird.*

- **4 teaspoons kosher or sea salt, divided**
- **2 cups reduced-sodium chicken broth**
- **⅓ cup dry sherry**
- **5 tablespoons salted butter, divided**
- **1 medium-size yellow onion, diced**
- **2 medium-size cloves garlic, minced**
- **4 cups (10 ounces) sliced button mushrooms**
- **1 small red bell pepper, seeded and diced**
- **½ teaspoon freshly grated nutmeg**
- **½ teaspoon paprika**
- **1 pound egg noodles**
- **3 tablespoons all-purpose flour**
- **½ cup milk**
- **¼ cup light cream**
- **½ cup grated Parmesan cheese**
- **2½ cups shredded cooked turkey (or chicken) breast (see "Note," above)**
- **Garnish: chopped fresh parsley**

1. Set a large pot of water over high heat and add 2 teaspoons salt.
2. In a small saucepan over medium-high heat, bring broth and sherry to a simmer.
3. In a large (14-inch) skillet, melt 2 tablespoons butter over medium heat. Add onion, garlic, mushrooms, red pepper, 1 teaspoon salt, nutmeg, and paprika; cook, stirring often, until vegetables soften, 8 to 10 minutes. Reduce heat to medium-low and continue cooking until golden brown, about 10 more minutes. Using a slotted spoon, transfer vegetables to a bowl and set aside.
4. Once water is boiling, add egg noodles. Cook according to package instructions until tender. Drain and set aside, covered.
5. Meanwhile, melt remaining butter in the skillet over medium heat. Add flour and cook, stirring until mixture looks glossy, about 3 minutes. Add broth and sherry mixture in a slow stream, whisking as you do. Bring to a simmer and cook until thickened, about 3 minutes. Remove from heat and add milk, cream, cheese, and remaining 1 teaspoon salt. Whisk together. Reduce heat to low, return pan to heat, and stir until thickened. Stir in vegetable mixture and cooked turkey (or chicken). Serve hot over noodles with a generous sprinkling of parsley.

BEEF STROGANOFF

*This Russian dish has been around for several centuries (*Larousse Gastronomique *dates it to the 1700s), but it wasn't until the 1940s and '50s that it became all the rage in the United States. Here's a delicious rendition that pays tribute to the "gourmet" chafing-dish dinner party. Now, as then, beef Stroganoff is a good thing to cook in front of a small crowd.*

TOTAL TIME: 45 MINUTES • **HANDS-ON TIME:** 45 MINUTES • **YIELD:** 6 SERVINGS

NOTE: *Tenderloin is the best cut of beef here, but a good cut of top sirloin can have excellent flavor and texture, if not as melt-in-your-mouth as the tenderloin.*

- 5 **teaspoons kosher or sea salt, divided**
- 1¾–2 **pounds beef tenderloin (see "Note," above)**
- 5 **tablespoons salted butter, divided**
- 1 **small yellow onion, minced**
- 10 **ounces (4 cups) sliced fresh button mushrooms**
- 1 **pound egg noodles**
- 2 **tablespoons all-purpose flour**
- 2 **cups reduced-sodium beef broth**
- 3 **tablespoons cognac or brandy**
- 1 **tablespoon Dijon mustard**
- 1 **teaspoon paprika**
- ¼ **teaspoon freshly ground black pepper**
- ¼ **teaspoon freshly ground nutmeg**
- 1 **cup sour cream, at room temperature**

1. Set a large pot of water to boil with 2 teaspoons salt.
2. Meanwhile, cut beef into slivers about 1½ inches long, ½ inch wide, and ¼ inch thick. Pat dry; then sprinkle with 1½ teaspoons salt. Melt 2 tablespoons butter in a large (14-inch) skillet over medium-high heat; then add half the beef. Sauté until seared, 4 to 7 minutes per batch; then transfer to a bowl. Repeat with remaining beef. Increase heat to high, add 2 tablespoons butter; then add onion, mushrooms, and remaining salt. Cook until mushrooms are lightly browned, about 5 minutes; then transfer to the bowl with beef.
3. Add noodles to the pot of boiling water and cook according to package instructions until tender. Drain and set aside, covered.
4. Add remaining butter and the flour to the skillet. Brown 3 minutes; then slowly whisk in broth. Remove from the heat and add cognac. Return to heat and whisk in mustard, paprika, pepper, and nutmeg. When sauce has thickened, turn the heat off and add sour cream. Add meat, onions, and mushrooms back into the pan and stir. Serve over noodles.

MAPLE-GLAZED SPARERIBS

These ribs are so finger-licking sticky good you may want to put finger bowls—warm water with lemon slices—on the table along with plenty of napkins for your guests. And don't be intimidated by making your own spice rub or barbecue glaze; it's as easy as stirring.

TOTAL TIME: 3½–4 HOURS • HANDS-ON TIME: 25 MINUTES • YIELD: 6 SERVINGS

FOR THE RIBS:

- 1   2½-pound rack baby back pork ribs
- 2   tablespoons firmly packed light-brown sugar
- 1   tablespoon paprika
- 1   tablespoon kosher or sea salt
- 1   tablespoon onion powder
- ⅛–¼   teaspoon cayenne pepper

FOR THE GLAZE:

- 1   tablespoon canola oil
- 1   tablespoon freshly minced garlic
- ¼   cup minced onion
- 2   tablespoons tomato paste
- 1   tablespoon cider vinegar
- 1   teaspoon Worcestershire sauce
- ½–1   teaspoon Tabasco sauce (optional)
- ⅛   teaspoon ground cloves
- ¾   cup maple syrup (any grade)
- ½   teaspoon kosher or sea salt

1. Rinse ribs with cold water and pat dry with paper towels. Cut between bones and arrange in a 13x9-inch baking dish.

2. Make the rub: In a small bowl, stir together brown sugar, paprika, salt, onion powder, and cayenne. Coat each rib with rub, cover with aluminum foil, and chill at least 2 hours (up to overnight).

3. Remove ribs from refrigerator, and preheat the oven to 350°. When hot, transfer ribs, covered with foil, to oven and bake 30 minutes.

4. Meanwhile, make the glaze: Put oil in a small saucepan over medium-high heat. Add garlic and onion; cook until translucent, 5 minutes. Add remaining ingredients. Whisk together; simmer over medium heat, stirring occasionally, 10 minutes.

5. Remove ribs from oven and turn. Cover and return to oven; bake 30 minutes more. Remove and baste with a third of the glaze, turning with tongs to coat. Return to oven uncovered, reduce heat to 325°, and bake until tender, 30 to 45 minutes more. Remove and coat with another third of the glaze. Serve with remaining glaze on the side.

SWEDISH MEATBALLS
(recipe on opposite page)

BELGIAN-STYLE PORK CARBONNADE

This hearty beer-and-onion stew is a national dish of Belgium and became very fashionable in the United States both in the 1970s and again more recently, thanks to the rise of the craft-beer movement. It's commonly made with beef, but this pork version is every bit as delicious. Choose a hoppy ale or lager—and bring home a few extras to tide you over during the three-hour braise. Serve over generously buttered egg noodles. The optional fresh horseradish root is worth seeking out.

TOTAL TIME: ABOUT 4 HOURS • HANDS-ON TIME: 45 MINUTES • YIELD: 6 TO 8 SERVINGS

8 ounces thick-cut bacon, coarsely chopped
6 sprigs fresh thyme, divided
3 tablespoons olive oil, divided
3 pounds boneless pork shoulder,
    trimmed and cut into 2-inch pieces, divided
1 tablespoon plus 1 teaspoon kosher or sea salt,
    plus more to taste
1 teaspoon freshly ground black pepper,
    plus more to taste
4 medium-size yellow onions, cut into ¼-inch slices
1 tablespoon granulated sugar
4 cloves garlic, minced
¼ cup all-purpose flour
1½ cups reduced-sodium chicken or beef broth
12 ounces Belgian-style beer
1 (14.5-ounce) can whole tomatoes, rinsed, drained,
    and roughly chopped
2 tablespoons apple cider vinegar
2 bay leaves
    Buttered egg noodles
    Garnish: ½ cup grated fresh horseradish root
    (optional)

1. Preheat the oven to 300°. Cook bacon and 1 thyme sprig in a large Dutch oven over medium heat until browned and crisped; with a slotted spoon, transfer to paper towels to drain, reserving fat in a separate bowl.
2. Heat 1 tablespoon reserved bacon fat and 1 tablespoon olive oil in the now-empty pan over medium-high heat. Thoroughly dry pork with paper towels, and season with 1 tablespoon salt and 1 teaspoon pepper. Cook half the pork, without moving the pieces, until well browned, 5 to 7 minutes, lowering heat if necessary to prevent burning; using tongs, flip the pieces and cook until the second side is browned, 5 to 7 minutes. Transfer pork and all juices to a large bowl. Repeat with 1 tablespoon bacon fat, 1 tablespoon olive oil, and remaining pork.
3. Heat remaining 1 tablespoon olive oil in the now-empty pan; add onions, sugar, and remaining 1 teaspoon salt; cook, stirring occasionally, until lightly browned, 12 to 14 minutes. Add garlic and continue cooking until fragrant, about 1 minute more. Add flour and cook until lightly browned, about 2 minutes more. Stir in broth, then beer, scraping the bottom of the pan with a wooden spoon. Add pork, tomatoes, vinegar, bay leaves, reserved bacon, and remaining thyme sprigs. Bring to a vigorous simmer, cover, and transfer to the lower-middle rack of the oven.
4. Cook 1 hour; remove cover, stir, and continue cooking, uncovered, until pork is fork-tender and sauce is thick, about 2 hours more. Remove from oven and let rest at least 20 minutes.
5. Remove thyme sprigs and bay leaves, adjust seasoning with salt and pepper, and serve over buttered egg noodles. Garnish with grated fresh horseradish, if you like.

QUAHOG FRITTERS WITH TARTAR SAUCE

For us Yankees, quahog fritters (if you're not from New England, quahogs are simply hard-shell clams) are the taste of summer at the Rhode Island or Connecticut shore. The dough absorbs the briny taste of the meat, and the tartar sauce gives it a sweet, zingy finish. You can easily halve the amounts for a smaller crowd.

TOTAL TIME: 35 MINUTES · **HANDS-ON TIME:** 35 MINUTES · **YIELD:** 6 TO 8 SERVINGS (ABOUT 3 DOZEN FRITTERS)

FOR THE SAUCE:
- ¾ cup mayonnaise
- ⅓ cup sweet relish, drained
- 2 tablespoons minced onion
- 1 teaspoon freshly grated lemon zest

FOR THE CLAMS:
- 2 pints shucked quahog meat, finely chopped (squeeze out and discard blacks)
- 1 medium-size onion, minced
- 2 small cloves garlic, minced
- 2 large eggs, lightly beaten
- ¼ cup vegetable oil, plus more for frying
- 1 cup all-purpose flour
- 1 teaspoon baking powder
- 2 teaspoons kosher or sea salt
- ½ teaspoon freshly ground black pepper

1. First, make the sauce: In a small bowl, stir together the four ingredients. Set aside.
2. Fill a 4- or 5-quart heavy-bottomed pot with 3 inches of oil and set over medium-high heat.
3. In a medium-size bowl, stir together quahogs, onion, garlic, eggs, and ¼ cup oil. Add flour, baking powder, salt, and pepper, and mix just until evenly combined. The batter should have the consistency of whipped cream. If it's too thick, add some quahog liquor or water. If it's too thin, add a bit more flour.
4. When oil temperature reaches 370°, drop the batter by the tablespoonful into the fat. Don't overcrowd the pot. When fritters are dark golden brown on both sides, 3 to 5 minutes total, transfer to paper towels to drain. Serve hot, with tartar sauce on the side.

BAKED SEA SCALLOPS WITH GARLIC & VERMOUTH

Contemporary cooks are fond of using red and white wines in their sauces and braises, but we rarely think to use vermouth these days, which is a shame. This fortified wine, flavored with a proprietary blend of herbs and barks, has a wonderfully concentrated flavor that goes well with seafood and poultry. Scallops and vermouth were a popular pairing in the 1950s and 1960s; in fact, both Craig Claiborne, then food editor of the New York Times, *and René Verdon, chef of the Kennedy White House, published cookbooks that featured scallops marinated in vermouth. The combination of butter, garlic, and vermouth in this sauce is heavenly—be sure to serve with lots of bread for mopping up the juices.*

TOTAL TIME: 45 MINUTES • **HANDS-ON TIME:** 20 MINUTES • **YIELD:** 4 TO 6 SERVINGS

NOTE: *If at all possible, seek out "dry" scallops for your cooking. They're pale beige in color and have a purer flavor. So-called "wet" scallops are kept in a phosphate solution that turns them milky white and makes them absorb water, thus diluting their sweetness.*

5	tablespoons salted butter, plus more for dish
2	pounds sea scallops (see "Note," above)
3	large cloves garlic, minced
3	tablespoons fresh lemon juice
2½	tablespoons dry vermouth
¼	cup grated Parmesan cheese
¾	cup panko breadcrumbs
½	teaspoon freshly ground black pepper
1½	teaspoons kosher or sea salt

1. Preheat the oven to 350°. Butter the bottom of a 9x13-inch baking dish. Wash scallops and pat dry. Arrange in a single layer in the dish and set aside.

2. Melt butter in a small skillet over medium-low heat. And garlic and cook until just translucent, about 1 minute. Remove from heat and stir in lemon juice and vermouth. Pour over scallops. Sprinkle cheese, panko, pepper, and salt over scallops. Bake until scallops are just translucent in the center, about 20 minutes. Serve with crusty bread to soak up the juices.

**BAKED SEA SCALLOPS
WITH GARLIC & VERMOUTH**
(recipe on opposite page)

NANCY CLANCY'S LINGUINE WITH RED CLAM SAUCE

Long a staple of red-sauce Italian restaurants, this vintage favorite is so easy and delicious that it should be in every cook's regular rotation.

TOTAL TIME: 40 MINUTES • **HANDS-ON TIME:** 40 MINUTES • **YIELD:** 4 TO 6 SERVINGS

¼ cup olive oil
3 tablespoons salted butter
6 cloves garlic, minced
¼ cup minced fresh parsley
3 tablespoons minced fresh basil
¼ cup grated Parmesan cheese, plus more for serving
Pinch red-pepper flakes
1 can (6 ounces) tomato paste
2 cans (6½ ounces each) minced clams with juice
½ cup water
1 tablespoon table salt (for pasta)
¾ pound linguini
Garnishes: chopped fresh basil leaves, grated Parmesan cheese

1. Combine oil and butter in a medium-size saucepan over medium heat. Add garlic and cook until just translucent, about 1 minute. Add herbs, cheese, red pepper, tomato paste, clams (with juice), and water. Bring to a simmer and cook, stirring occasionally, for 20 minutes. If the sauce seems too thick, add another 1 to 2 tablespoons of water.
2. Meanwhile, bring a large pot of water to a boil over high heat. Add salt. Add pasta and cook according to package instructions until just tender. Drain pasta, put in a serving bowl, and top with sauce. Garnish with basil and serve with extra Parmesan.

LOBSTER PIE

Lobster pie has long been a popular way to serve our favorite crustacean. This one is a classic, loaded as it is with butter and sherry to bring out the meat's natural sweetness. A cracker topping gives it a pleasant crunch.

TOTAL TIME: 40 MINUTES • **HANDS-ON TIME:** 40 MINUTES • **YIELD:** 4 SERVINGS

FOR THE TOPPING:
½ cup finely crushed Ritz or other buttery crackers
½ teaspoon paprika
2 tablespoons grated Parmesan cheese
4 tablespoons salted butter, melted

FOR THE FILLING:
3 tablespoons plus 5 tablespoons salted butter
½ cup good-quality dry sherry
2 cups chopped cooked lobster meat
2 tablespoons all-purpose flour
1½ cups half-and-half
4 large egg yolks

(recipe continues on next page)

1. Preheat the oven to 350°. Make the topping: In a small bowl, stir together crackers, paprika, and cheese. Stir in 4 tablespoons butter until evenly mixed. Set aside.
2. Make the filling: In a 2- to 3-quart pot over medium-high heat, melt 3 tablespoons butter. Add sherry and boil 1 minute. Add lobster, stir, and remove from heat.
3. In a medium-size saucepan over medium heat, melt remaining 5 tablespoons butter. Add flour and cook, stirring, until mixture looks smooth and glossy. Remove from heat. With a slotted spoon, remove lobster from liquid and set aside. Add sherry mixture and half-and-half to butter/flour mixture. Return to heat and cook, stirring continuously, until sauce is smooth and thick.
4. Spoon ¼ cup of the sauce into a small bowl. Add egg yolks one at a time, beating well after each addition (see p. 181, top). Return egg mixture to sauce and mix well. Stir over low heat until thickened, about 3 minutes; don't let it boil. Remove from heat and add lobster. Pour mixture into four ramekins or a gratin dish. Sprinkle with topping. Bake until golden brown, 10 to 15 minutes.

PORTUGUESE FISHERMAN'S STEW (*CALDEIRADA À PESCADORA*)

Here's a seafood casserole that isn't heavy or gloppy in the least. Based on a traditional Portuguese dish, it layers onion, white fish, potatoes, and tomatoes in a white wine broth—a symphony of harmonious flavors.

TOTAL TIME: 1 HOUR 10 MINUTES • HANDS-ON TIME: 35 MINUTES • YIELD: 6 TO 8 SERVINGS

½ cup olive oil
4 large onions, sliced
2 large cloves garlic, minced
½ bunch fresh parsley leaves, minced
2 teaspoons kosher or sea salt, divided
½ teaspoon freshly ground black pepper
½ teaspoon ground coriander seed
2 pounds white fish, such as haddock, flounder, or cod
6 medium-size russet potatoes, peeled and sliced ¼ inch thick
1 28-ounce can diced tomatoes
1 bay leaf
1 cup dry white wine, such as Pinot Grigio

1. Set a 4- to 5-quart heavy-bottomed pot over medium heat. Add the oil. When sizzling, add the onions, garlic, parsley, 1 teaspoon salt, pepper, and coriander. Cook, stirring occasionally, until the onions are golden, 10 to 12 minutes.
2. Place the fish in an even layer over the onions; then layer in the potatoes, tomatoes, bay leaf, remaining 1 teaspoon salt, and wine. Cover tightly, reduce heat to low, and gently simmer until the potatoes are done and the fish is cooked through, 35 to 45 minutes. Remove bay leaf before serving.

WORLD'S BEST STICKY BUNS
(recipe on page 86)

Breakfasts and Breads

These recipes come to us from the era when breakfast was designed to fuel a day's worth of work and bread was something you made, not bought. Today, we toss back cereal or grab a yogurt on our way out the door, and we celebrate the folks who do the kneading and baking for us. But weekends are the time to savor homemade creations like crumb coffee cake, an updated red flannel hash, lingonberry pancakes, sticky buns, and potato doughnuts. Potato doughnuts, you might ask? Yes, and they may well be the most tender and delicious you've ever had.

SCOTCH EGGS

The first recorded recipe for Scotch eggs is from an 1807 book, A New System of Domestic Cookery, Formed Upon Principles of Economy, and Adapted to the Use of Private Families *by Maria Eliza Rundell, a British domestic expert, the Martha Stewart of her day. It was (and remains) popular pub fare, but we think it makes a wonderful breakfast served with toast. How long the eggs need to fry in oil depends on the kind of sausage meat used: Turkey and chicken cook through faster than pork.*

TOTAL TIME: 45 MINUTES • HANDS-ON TIME: 20 TO 25 MINUTES • YIELD: 6 EGGS

8 **large eggs, divided**
½ **cup all-purpose flour**
   Kosher or sea salt and freshly ground black pepper,
      to taste
½ **pound sausage meat, bulk**
      or removed from individual link casings
½ **cup panko breadcrumbs**
½ **cup freshly grated Parmesan cheese**
   Vegetable oil (for deep-fat frying)

1. Par-cook 6 eggs: Put in a small pot, cover with water, and set over high heat. Bring to a boil. Turn off heat, keep covered, and let eggs sit for 7 minutes. Transfer to an ice-water bath to cool. Peel; then set aside.
2. Beat the 2 remaining uncooked eggs in a small bowl.
3. Mix the flour, salt, and pepper together on a piece of wax paper. Divide the sausage meat into 6 equal parts; then press the sausage down into thin patties. Dip each of the 6 cooked eggs into the beaten eggs, roll in the flour mixture, and wrap with sausage, pressing firmly to adhere. You'll use roughly half the beaten eggs for this step.
4. Combine the panko and grated cheese on a plate.
5. Brush the remaining beaten egg equally over the sausage-coated eggs and then roll each egg in the panko/cheese mixture.
6. Meanwhile, heat 2 to 3 inches of oil in a deep frying pan to about 375°. Deep-fry the eggs in the oil until golden brown, turning the eggs for even cooking, 5 to 7 minutes. Drain on paper towels and serve.

RED FLANNEL HASH CASSEROLE

This beloved New England staple, traditionally made with the leftovers from a boiled dinner, takes on new life with the addition of a goat's-milk cheese custard on top. Pancetta, Italian bacon now widely available in many supermarkets, makes an easy substitute for traditional bacon. But you can substitute 6 slices of bacon instead, if you choose.

TOTAL TIME: 1 HOUR 30 MINUTES · **HANDS-ON TIME:** 30 MINUTES · **YIELD:** 4 MAIN-COURSE SERVINGS

4 ounces diced pancetta (or 6 slices bacon, chopped)
1 large onion, finely chopped
2 medium-size cloves garlic, minced
3 cups diced cooked roast beef and/or corned beef
2 cups diced cooked potatoes
2 cups diced cooked beets
2 large eggs, beaten
1 cup whole milk
4 ounces fresh goat cheese (chèvre),
    at room temperature
Kosher or sea salt and freshly ground black pepper,
    to taste

1. In a medium-size (10- to 12-inch) skillet over medium heat, cook the pancetta until it begins to brown, 4 to 5 minutes. Stir in the onion and garlic and cook until onion is soft, 6 to 7 minutes. Remove from heat.
2. Preheat the oven to 350°.
3. Combine the beef, potatoes, and beets in a 3-quart ovenproof casserole. Stir in the pancetta/onion mixture. Transfer casserole to the oven and bake, uncovered, for 30 minutes.
4. Meanwhile, in a mixing bowl, stir the eggs with the milk. Add the goat cheese, mashing it into the milk and eggs. Season with salt and pepper. After the beef/potato mixture has baked for 30 minutes, pour the goat-cheese mixture over the hash and return to the oven. Bake until the top has crisped, 15 to 20 minutes longer. Remove from oven and let rest a couple of minutes; then slice and serve.

SHIRRED EGGS & HAM

Recipes for eggs seasoned and baked in an earthenware dish were popular in 19th-century cookbooks, including Fannie Farmer's original Boston Cooking-School Cook Book. *The name for this recipe comes from the flat-bottomed dish, or "shirrer," in which they were traditionally cooked. These days, shirred eggs are usually baked in ramekins. But in this fantastic brunch variation, we line muffin cups with thin slices of ham and then drop in the eggs before baking. It's a fast, pretty, and delicious way to serve breakfast for a crowd.*

TOTAL TIME: 45 MINUTES • HANDS-ON TIME: 45 MINUTES • YIELD: 6 SERVINGS

12 pieces thinly sliced ham

12 medium-size eggs

12 teaspoons heavy cream

2 tablespoons grated Parmesan cheese

Zest of 1 lemon

6 teaspoons pimentos, drained (optional)

Freshly ground black pepper, to taste

Garnish: 4 strands fresh chive

Boiling water

1. Preheat the oven to 325° and bring a kettleful of water to a simmer. Mist 12 muffin cups with nonstick cooking spray. Line each cup with a slice of ham. Into each cup crack 1 egg; add 1 teaspoon cream, a sprinkling of Parmesan cheese, a pinch of zest, and ½ teaspoon pimentos. Add pepper to taste (the ham and cheese provide enough salt). Using scissors, snip a little chive over each cup.

2. Set a baking dish (large enough to hold the muffin tins) on a rack in the middle of the oven, and pour 1 inch of the simmering water into the dish. Set the muffin pan into the water bath and bake eggs until whites are opaque, 12 to 15 minutes. Serve warm.

SHIRRED EGGS & HAM
(recipe on opposite page)

BLUEBERRY BOY BAIT
(recipe on opposite page)

BLUEBERRY BOY BAIT

In 1954 a 15-year-old Chicago girl named Renny Powell submitted a blueberry coffee cake recipe to the "Pillsbury $100,000 Recipe & Baking Contest" (precursor to today's "Pillsbury Bake-Off"). Renny took second place in the youth division for her creation, named in honor of its powers with the opposite sex. The recipe has been in circulation for nearly 60 years now, including on YankeeMagazine.com, where our adaptation is one of the most popular recipes in our archive.

TOTAL TIME: 1 HOUR 10 MINUTES • **HANDS-ON TIME:** 20 MINUTES • **YIELD:** 18 SQUARES

FOR THE CAKE:

Butter (for the pan)
2 cups all-purpose flour
1 cup granulated sugar
2 teaspoons baking powder
¼ teaspoon table salt
⅔ cup vegetable oil
1 cup milk
2 large eggs
3 cups blueberries, fresh or frozen

FOR THE TOPPING:

3 tablespoons granulated sugar
1 teaspoon ground cinnamon

1. Preheat the oven to 350° and butter a 9x13-inch baking pan. Set an oven rack to the middle position.
2. In a medium-size bowl, whisk together the flour, sugar, baking powder, and salt. Add the oil, milk, and eggs. Mix with an electric mixer until well combined.
3. Pour the batter into the prepared pan; then evenly sprinkle the blueberries on top.
4. In a small bowl, combine the sugar and cinnamon; then sprinkle over the blueberries. Bake until a cake tester inserted into the center comes out clean, about 50 minutes.

WORLD'S BEST STICKY BUNS

Everybody loves sticky buns. These beauties, bolstered by rolled oats and energized by a couple of shots of maple syrup, are hard to beat. While they're beloved for breakfast, there's no reason you can't serve them warm, with a scoop of vanilla ice cream or a dollop of whipped cream, for dessert.

TOTAL TIME: 3½ TO 4 HOURS · **HANDS-ON TIME:** 35 TO 40 MINUTES · **YIELD:** 1 DOZEN

FOR THE DOUGH:

- ¼ cup warm water
- 1 package (scant tablespoon) active dry yeast
- ¾ cup rolled oats
- ⅓ cup granulated sugar
- 1¼ cups whole milk, heated
- 2 large eggs, at room temperature
- 2 large egg yolks, at room temperature
- ¼ cup unsalted butter, softened, plus more for bowl
-   Finely grated zest of 1 lemon
- 2 teaspoons vanilla extract
- 1 teaspoon maple syrup
- 2 teaspoons kosher or sea salt
- 4½ cups unbleached all-purpose flour, divided, plus more for work surface

FOR THE SYRUP AND FILLING:

- ½ cup (1 stick) plus 3 tablespoons unsalted butter, melted, divided
- 1¼ cups light-brown sugar, packed, divided
- 2 teaspoons cinnamon
- 2 tablespoons maple syrup
- 1 cup chopped walnuts, lightly toasted and cooled

1. Pour the water into a small bowl and sprinkle the yeast over it. Set aside.
2. Combine the oats and sugar in a very large bowl. Pour in the heated milk, stirring to dissolve the sugar. Set aside for 5 minutes.

3. Whisk eggs and egg yolks together in a small bowl; then add them to the oat/sugar mixture. Add ¼ cup butter, along with the lemon zest, vanilla, 1 teaspoon of maple syrup, and the salt. Gently stir in the dissolved yeast. Add 3½ cups of the flour; beat vigorously 100 strokes. Set aside for 10 minutes.
4. After the dough has rested, gradually add the remaining 1 cup flour until a soft, kneadable dough forms. Turn the dough out onto a lightly floured surface and knead for 5 to 6 minutes. Use just enough flour to keep the dough from sticking.
5. Place the dough in a lightly buttered bowl and cover with plastic wrap. Set aside in a warm, draft-free spot until it doubles in bulk (at least 90 minutes, and up to 2 hours).
6. Next, make the syrup: Brush ½ cup melted butter over the sides and the bottoms of two 10-inch round cake pans or ovenproof skillets. Sprinkle each pan with ½ cup brown sugar. Set aside.
7. Pour the remaining ¼ cup brown sugar, cinnamon, maple syrup, and walnuts into the bowl of a food processor and pulse a few times.
8. Dust your work area with flour and turn dough out onto it. Don't punch it down. Roll the dough into a 12x18-inch rectangle, keeping the long side facing you. Push it down lightly. Brush with the remaining 3 tablespoons melted butter and spread half the brown sugar/walnut mixture over the dough, leaving a 1-inch border at the top; set aside the remaining brown sugar/walnut mixture. Starting with the long side facing you, roll the dough up snugly.

(recipe continues on next page)

9. Using a sharp knife, cut the dough into 12 slices and lay them in the prepared pans or skillets, spiral side up. You'll fit 6 in each pan, with 1 in the center and 5 in a circle all around. Gently pat down the spirals. Cover the pans or skillets with plastic and set aside in a warm area until the buns have almost doubled in size, about 45 minutes.

10. Preheat the oven to 375°. Bake for 25 minutes. Top each bun evenly with the remaining brown sugar/walnut mixture; then return to the oven and bake for 5 to 6 more minutes, or until golden brown. Remove from the oven and turn the buns out onto a baking sheet to cool for 10 to 15 minutes. Serve warm or at room temperature.

SOUR CREAM COFFEE CAKE

As food historian Lynne Olver notes on her wonderful site, FoodTimeline.org, *coffee cakes like these weren't invented—they evolved. Sweet cakes made to be served with coffee first began to appear in the 17th century, when coffee was introduced to Northern Europe. But this style of cake, enriched with sour cream and bisected by a layer of streusel, became especially popular in the United States in the 1950s and 1960s and remains a favorite today.*

TOTAL TIME: 1 HOUR · **HANDS-ON TIME:** 20 MINUTES · **YIELD:** 10 SERVINGS

⅓ **cup chopped walnuts**

⅓ **cup firmly packed light-brown sugar**

1 **teaspoon ground cinnamon**

2 **cups sifted all-purpose flour**

1 **teaspoon baking powder**

1 **teaspoon baking soda**

½ **teaspoon table salt**

½ **cup salted butter, softened, plus more for pan**

1 **cup granulated sugar**

2 **large eggs**

1 **teaspoon vanilla extract**

1 **cup sour cream**

1. Preheat the oven to 350° and grease a 6-cup tube pan. Set aside.

2. Make the topping: Stir together the walnuts, brown sugar, and cinnamon, and set aside.

3. Whisk the flour with the baking powder, baking soda, and salt until well combined. Cream the butter with the granulated sugar until the mixture is fluffy and light, 3 to 4 minutes; then beat in the eggs and vanilla. Add the flour mixture in alternating thirds with the sour cream, beating well after each addition.

4. Spoon half the batter into the pan and sprinkle with half the topping; then add the remaining batter and sprinkle on the rest of the topping. Bake for 40 minutes without opening the oven; then test for doneness (a toothpick should come out clean) and bake for 5 to 10 more minutes, if needed.

CRUMB COFFEE CAKE

Like sour cream coffee cake, crumb cake was a Northern European invention, originally prepared with a yeast-raised dough but simplified in the 20th century with the use of chemical leaveners such as baking powder. It's generally thought of as a New York specialty, but it's found all across New England as well.

TOTAL TIME: 45 MINUTES • **HANDS-ON TIME:** 20 MINUTES • **YIELD:** 9 SERVINGS

FOR THE CRUMB TOPPING:
- ¾ cup all-purpose flour
- ½ cup packed light-brown sugar
- ⅓ cup chopped walnuts
- 2 teaspoons ground cinnamon
- ½ cup (1 stick) salted butter, melted

FOR THE CAKE:
- 1½ cups all-purpose flour
- ¾ cup granulated sugar
- 1 tablespoon baking powder
- ½ teaspoon table salt
- ¼ cup (½ stick) salted butter, melted, plus more for pan
- 1 large egg
- ½ cup milk
- 1 teaspoon vanilla extract

1. Preheat the oven to 375° and grease an 8-inch square baking pan.
2. Make the crumb topping: Combine the flour, brown sugar, walnuts, and cinnamon. Add the melted butter and mix with a fork. Set aside.
3. Next, make the cake: In a large bowl, whisk together the flour, sugar, baking powder, and salt. In a medium-size bowl, whisk together the butter, egg, milk, and vanilla. Add the wet mixture to the dry ingredients and fold with a rubber spatula until just combined. Spread the batter evenly in the prepared pan. Top with the crumb topping. Bake until a toothpick inserted into the center comes out clean, 25 to 30 minutes.

CRUMB COFFEE CAKE
(recipe on opposite page)

JOHNNYCAKES

In the earliest days of the American colonies, ground cornmeal was used as a substitute for harder-to-find wheat flours. Native Americans taught the Europeans how to combine it with boiled water to make a simple batter, and they, in turn, added milk, molasses, and butter for various cakes and puddings. Johnnycakes (also spelled johnny cakes *and* jonnycakes*) were one of those variations. Every October, Kenyon's Grist Mill in Usquepaugh, Rhode Island, hosts a festival celebrating this heritage food.*

TOTAL TIME: 25 MINUTES • **HANDS-ON TIME:** 25 MINUTES • **YIELD:** ABOUT 12 CAKES

NOTE: *For thin, crisp cakes, omit the boiling water, increase the milk to 1¾ cups, and reduce the cooking time to 3 to 4 minutes on each side. Whitecap flint cornmeal, made by Kenyon's and by Gray's Grist Mill in Westport, Massachusetts, is available in many stores around New England. You may substitute regular yellow cornmeal (though the results aren't quite as authentic).*

1	cup whitecap flint cornmeal (see "Note," above)
½	teaspoon kosher or sea salt
2	teaspoons granulated sugar
1½	cups boiling water
3	tablespoons whole milk
3–4	tablespoons unsalted butter, divided

1. In a medium-size bowl, whisk together cornmeal, salt, and sugar. Whisk in boiling water until mixture has the consistency of loose mashed potatoes. Whisk in milk. The batter will thicken as it cools.
2. Melt half the butter on a skillet over medium-high heat. Pour large spoonfuls (about 3 tablespoons each) of batter onto the skillet and brown, about 5 minutes on each side. Repeat with remaining batter and butter. Serve hot with maple syrup.

STUMP JUMPER'S BUCKWHEAT CAKE

Looking for something different and delicious for breakfast? Try this cake that stands in for bread, bagels, or muffins, and craves a swirl of local honey or maple syrup. The origin of the name isn't readily known, but we suspect it may refer to New England's venerable logging tradition.

TOTAL TIME: 50 TO 55 MINUTES • **HANDS-ON TIME:** 15 TO 20 MINUTES • **YIELD:** 1 LOAF

½ cup granulated sugar
½ cup all-purpose flour
1 teaspoon baking soda
¾ teaspoon table salt
1¼ cup buckwheat flour
1 cup buttermilk
5 tablespoons unsalted butter, melted
1 large egg, beaten
Butter (for baking pan), plus more for serving
Honey or maple syrup (for serving)

1. Preheat the oven to 425°.
2. Sift sugar, all-purpose flour, baking soda, salt, and buckwheat flour into a large mixing bowl. Gradually stir in the buttermilk; then stir in the melted butter and beaten egg. Using an electric mixer, beat at medium speed until smooth.
3. Grease a 9-inch cake pan or 8-inch square baking pan with butter. Pour the batter into the pan.
4. Transfer to oven and bake for 35 minutes, or until a toothpick inserted into the cake comes out clean. Serve with butter and honey or maple syrup.

LINGONBERRY PANCAKES

Interest in Scandinavian culture, design, and cooking ran high in the 1960s, and these crêpe-like pancakes filled with lingonberry preserves were a popular brunch or dessert item. The fruits themselves resemble small cranberries, and they're wonderfully tart.

TOTAL TIME: 1 HOUR 25 MINUTES • **HANDS-ON TIME:** 45 MINUTES • **YIELD:** 12 PANCAKES

NOTE: *Lingonberry preserves are available at Ikea stores, gourmet shops, and most supermarkets with a good international aisle. You may also substitute currant jam, sour-cherry preserves, or raspberry jam.*

- **4** large eggs, lightly beaten
- **3** tablespoons granulated sugar
- **¾** cup heavy cream
- **2¼** cups milk
- **1¼** cups all-purpose flour
- **½** teaspoon table salt
- **4** tablespoons unsalted butter, melted, plus more for skillet
- **¾** teaspoon vanilla extract
- **Lingonberry preserves (see "Note," above)**
- **Garnish: powdered sugar**

1. In a 6-cup blender, whir eggs briefly. Add sugar, cream, and milk, and blend. Add flour and salt, and blend 5 seconds. The batter will seem loose; don't worry. Add melted butter and vanilla, and blend, first on low, then going up to medium, until emulsified, about 30 seconds. Let batter rest at least 30 minutes (or up to overnight).

2. Melt about 1 teaspoon butter in a heavy-bottomed skillet over medium-low heat. Ladle ½ cup batter into the pan and swirl to form a thin circle. Cook until pancake is lightly browned on bottom and cooked through on top, 3 to 5 minutes (no need to flip).

3. Spoon preserves down the center and roll the sides up and over, like a crêpe. Sprinkle with powdered sugar. Repeat with remaining batter and preserves.

LINGONBERRY PANCAKES
(recipe on opposite page)

DANISH CHRISTMAS WREATHS

We'll admit it: This recipe is a project, a special-occasion treat you may make once in your life, or once a year at Christmas. (Or maybe never—but isn't it still fun to learn how it's made?) If you have the patience to follow along, you'll be rewarded with one of the most delicious pastries you'll ever eat—a buttery, flaky dough filled with sweet almond paste.

Interestingly, Danish pastries aren't really a Danish invention. The Danes call them "Wienerbrod," or "Viennese bread," and they do closely resemble the signature yeast pastries of Austria. But for some reason, the Austrians associated the pastry with Scandinavia and the name stuck.

TOTAL TIME: 8 HOURS 30 MINUTES • **HANDS-ON TIME:** 1 HOUR 30 MINUTES • **YIELD:** 2 WREATHS

FOR THE DOUGH:
- ¾ **cup whole milk**
- ½ **cup granulated sugar**
- 1½ **teaspoons kosher or sea salt**
- 1¾ **cups unsalted butter (3½ sticks), divided**
- ¼ **cup lukewarm water (105° to 115°)**
- 2 **packages (scant tablespoon each) active dry yeast**
- 3 **large eggs, beaten, at room temperature**
- 4½ **cups flour, divided, plus more for dusting**

FOR THE ALMOND FILLING:
- 7 **ounces almond paste**
- ¾ **cup crushed zwieback (available in the baby-food aisle) or similar cookie**
- ½ **cup salted butter, melted**
- 1 **large egg, beaten**
- ½ **teaspoon almond extract**

FOR THE GLAZE:
- 1 **cup confectioners' sugar**
- 2 **tablespoons water**
- **Garnish: candied fruits (optional)**

1. First make the dough: Combine milk, sugar, salt, and ¼ cup (½ stick) butter in a small pot over high heat. Bring just to the simmering point; then remove from heat and cool to about 110°. In a large bowl or standing mixer, dissolve yeast in lukewarm water. Add the cooled milk mixture, the eggs, and 1 cup flour; beat well. Gradually add the remaining flour and continue to mix until a smooth dough forms. Transfer the dough to a large greased bowl and flip to coat; then cover with plastic wrap and chill 2 hours.

2. While dough is chilling, let 1½ cups (3 sticks) butter soften to room temperature; then roll out into a 10x12-inch rectangle between two sheets of parchment or waxed paper. (You may find it easier to first cut each stick into fourths lengthwise and lay the pieces in a row at the center of the parchment, before rolling.) Refrigerate until ready to use.

3. On a floured surface, roll dough out into a 10x20-inch rectangle (approximately). Peel the parchment or paper from the chilled butter and cover the bottom two-thirds of the dough with the butter; then fold into thirds, folding the unbuttered third of the dough toward the center first. Rotate the dough 90°; then roll out and fold into thirds again. Wrap loosely in parchment paper and chill for 1 hour.

4. Roll out again, fold into thirds, and chill briefly. Repeat this process twice more. After the fourth "turn," chill at least 3 hours, or overnight. As long as the dough is well wrapped, it can keep up to 1 week in the refrigerator. *Note:* When working with this dough, make sure the room is cool. If the butter starts to ooze, sprinkle the work surface with more flour and chill the dough periodically. *(recipe continues on next page)*

5. Next, make the filling: Mix ingredients together until smooth, and set aside, keeping cool.

6. Divide dough in half and return one half to the fridge, loosely wrapped in parchment. Roll out the first batch of dough into a rectangle 8x22 inches and cut into 3 long strips. Transfer 1 cup of almond filling to a large, heavy-duty zip-top bag and snip off one corner. Pipe a thick line of almond filling down the center of each strip. Pinch the edges of the dough together over the filling, rolling the dough seam-side down as you go, to keep the filling sealed.

7. Braid the three strands of dough together on a sheet of parchment, arranging into a wreath about 14 inches in diameter.

8. Repeat this process with the remaining dough and almond filling. Let wreaths rise for 1 hour.

9. About 15 minutes before you're ready to bake the wreaths, preheat the oven to 375°. Bake until golden, about 30 minutes.

10. Transfer to a wire rack to cool. While wreaths are cooling, make the glaze: Stir the water into the confectioners' sugar until smooth. Decorate cooled wreaths with glaze and candied fruits, if you like.

SALLY LUNN

This delicate tea cake has been in existence since the late 18th century, but its exact origins are a matter of debate. Some records state that Sally Lunn was a real person, a baker in Bath, England, whose cakes brought her wide acclaim among the tourists who took the waters in that spa town. Others say the name derives from the French soleil et lune, *or "sun and moon" cake. It's a puzzle. In the earliest recipes, yeast was used as the leavening agent, and the dough was baked in the form of small, individual cakes. Our recipe is much simpler, as the batter is made with baking powder and poured into a single loaf pan for baking.*

TOTAL TIME: 1 HOUR 5 MINUTES • **HANDS-ON TIME:** 20 MINUTES • **YIELD:** 15 SLICES

2 **large eggs, separated, at room temperature**
2 **cups all-purpose flour**
1 **tablespoon baking powder**
½ **teaspoon table salt**
¼ **cup granulated sugar**
⅔ **cup milk**
½ **cup salted butter, melted, plus more for pan**

1. Preheat the oven to 375° and grease a 9x5-inch loaf pan.

2. In a clean bowl, beat the egg whites to firm peaks and set aside. Whisk together the dry ingredients and set aside.

3. In a small bowl, whisk together the milk and egg yolks. Add to the dry ingredients, stirring until just combined. Stir in the melted butter; then fold in the stiffly beaten egg whites.

4. Pour into the prepared pan and bake until a toothpick inserted into the center comes out clean, about 45 minutes. (Tent the pan with foil after 30 minutes if the top is browning too fast).

POTATO DOUGHNUTS

Potato doughnuts reached the status of food fad in the 1940s, when Al and Bob Pelton of Salt Lake City, Utah, launched the "Spudnut" bakery craze, with chains in more than 30 states. Meanwhile, in Maine potato country, home cooks had developed their own doughnuts, a popular way to serve potatoes for breakfast. A few Spudnut shops remain in Southern and Western states, and The Holy Donut Shop in Portland, Maine, serves more than a dozen flavors, all made with potatoes. But if you can't get there, it's worth making your own.

TOTAL TIME: 1 HOUR 30 MINUTES • **HANDS-ON TIME:** 40 MINUTES • **YIELD:** 3 DOZEN

NOTE: *For best results, pass the potatoes through a ricer or food mill. It makes the texture fluffier.*

- 1 **pound russet potatoes (about 2 large potatoes)**
- 1 **cup milk**
- 2 **cups granulated sugar**
- 4 **large eggs**
- 4 **tablespoons salted butter, melted**
- 6 **cups all-purpose flour, plus more for work surface and as needed**
- 2 **tablespoons baking powder**
- 1 **teaspoon ground nutmeg**
- ¼ **teaspoon ground cinnamon**
- ½ **teaspoon table salt**
- 1½ **quarts vegetable oil (for frying)**
- **Garnish: cinnamon sugar**

1. Peel the potatoes; cut into large chunks. Put potatoes in a medium-size pot and cover with water. Set over high heat and bring to a boil; then reduce heat to a simmer and cook until tender, about 30 minutes. Drain, then pass potatoes through a ricer or food mill, and cool to room temperature.

2. In the bowl of a standing mixer or, if using a hand-held mixer, in a large bowl, beat potatoes with milk. Add sugar and beat well; then add eggs one at a time, beating well after each. Add butter and beat.

3. In a separate bowl, whisk together flour, baking powder, spices, and salt. Add to wet ingredients and stir with a spatula, just until dry ingredients are evenly moistened. Dough should be moist but workable. If it doesn't come together, add more flour, ¼ cup at a time. Turn dough out onto a well-floured surface and knead two or three times. Press out to a ¾-inch thickness. Dust with flour, cover with a towel, and let sit for 15 minutes.

4. Meanwhile, in a Dutch oven or another large, heavy-bottomed pot, heat the vegetable oil to 370°.

5. Using a well-floured 2½-inch doughnut cutter or two concentric biscuit cutters, cut out 36 doughnuts, gathering and rerolling dough as needed. Fry, 4 to 6 at a time to avoid crowding, until golden brown on both sides and cooked through, 2½ to 3 minutes each. Sprinkle with cinnamon sugar.

POTATO DOUGHNUTS
(recipe on opposite page)

VERMONT APPLE-CIDER DOUGHNUTS

It's a cider maker's tradition to use some of the freshly pressed juice to make lightly tangy, apple-scented doughnuts like these. The cider adds more than flavor, though; its acidity makes the doughnuts more tender.

TOTAL TIME: 1 HOUR 45 MINUTES • **HANDS-ON TIME:** 1 HOUR 30 MINUTES • **YIELD:** ABOUT 18 3-INCH DOUGHNUTS

NOTE: *Boiled apple cider gives these doughnuts a rich, slightly tangy flavor. You can buy boiled cider at some gourmet and Whole Foods stores; from Wood's Cider Mill in Springfield, Vermont* (woodscidermill.com); *or from the King Arthur Flour catalogue. Alternatively, you can boil your own by simmering 1½ cups of fresh apple cider down to ⅓ cup in about 25 minutes; it just won't be as concentrated as the commercial product.*

- 1 **cup granulated sugar**
- 5 **tablespoons unsalted butter, at room temperature**
- 2 **large eggs, at room temperature**
- 3½–4 **cups all-purpose flour, plus more for work surface**
- 1¼ **teaspoons table salt**
- 2 **teaspoons baking powder**
- 1 **teaspoon baking soda**
- 1½ **teaspoons ground cinnamon**
- ½ **teaspoon freshly grated nutmeg**
- ½ **cup low-fat buttermilk**
- ⅓ **cup boiled apple cider**
- 1 **tablespoon vanilla extract**
  Canola or safflower oil (for frying)
  Cinnamon sugar (1½ cups sugar mixed with
  3 tablespoons ground cinnamon)
  or confectioners' sugar

1. In a large bowl using a handheld or standing mixer fitted with a whisk attachment, beat together sugar and butter until mixture is pale and fluffy, 4 to 6 minutes. Add eggs, one at a time, beating a minute after each. Set aside. In a medium-size bowl, whisk together 3½ cups flour, salt, baking powder, baking soda, cinnamon, and nutmeg; set aside.

2. Pour buttermilk, boiled cider, and vanilla into sugar/butter/egg mixture. Mix well, and don't worry if the mixture looks a bit curdled; it will smooth itself out. Add flour mixture and combine gently just until fully moistened. If dough seems loose, add additional flour, 2 tablespoons at a time, until it's firm enough to work with.

3. Line two baking sheets with waxed paper or parchment paper and dust generously with flour. Turn dough out onto one baking sheet and pat gently into ¾-inch thickness. Sprinkle dough with additional flour, cover with plastic wrap, and place in the freezer for 10 minutes to firm up. Remove dough from the freezer; use a lightly floured 3-inch doughnut cutter (or two concentric biscuit cutters) to cut out about 18 doughnuts with holes. (Gather the scraps and roll again as needed, but you may need to chill the dough more to firm it up.) Place cut doughnuts on the other baking sheet as you go; then transfer to the freezer for 5 minutes to firm up again.

4. Line a plate with a few layers of paper towels and set it nearby. In a Dutch oven or large pot, heat 3 inches of oil to 370° (test with an instant-read thermometer). Drop 3 or 4 doughnuts into the oil, being careful not to crowd the pan. Cook until browned on one side, about 1 minute; then flip and cook until browned on the other side, about 1 minute longer.

5. Repeat with the remaining dough. (If you find that it's getting too soft as you work your way through the batches, pop it into the freezer again for 10 minutes.) When doughnuts are cool enough to handle but still warm, sprinkle all over with cinnamon sugar or confectioners' sugar. Serve immediately.

ANADAMA BREAD

The name "anadama bread" first appeared in print in 1915, but it was undoubtedly baked in many New England hearths before then. What distinguishes anadama from other breads is the inclusion of cornmeal and molasses. Both were common ingredients in Northeast cooking, but they truly shine in this bread. So what does "anadama" mean? Local legend overwhelmingly credits a Gloucester fisherman with coining the term as a not-so-loving tribute to his wife, Anna. It seems Anna wasn't blessed with talent in the kitchen, and after numerous bowls of molasses and cornmeal porridge for supper, the fisherman angrily tossed in some flour and yeast one evening and threw the mixture into the oven. While it baked, he sat muttering, "Anna, damn her!" and the name was born. Fortunately, so was this delicious bread. The molasses and cornmeal make for a sweet and nutty aroma while it bakes, which carries over into the flavor.

TOTAL TIME: 3 HOURS 30 MINUTES • HANDS-ON TIME: 40 MINUTES • YIELD: 3 LOAVES

2 tablespoons vegetable oil (for bowl), plus more for pans

2 packages (scant tablespoon each) active dry yeast

½ cup lukewarm water

2 cups milk

1 cup yellow cornmeal

⅔ cup molasses

3 tablespoons salted butter, melted

1½ teaspoons table salt

7–8 cups bread or all-purpose flour

1. Grease a large mixing bowl and set aside. Grease three 9x5-inch loaf pans and set aside. Dissolve the yeast in water and set aside. In another large bowl, combine milk, cornmeal, molasses, butter, and salt. Add 4 cups flour and the yeast mixture and stir to form a dough. Add remaining flour a bit at a time, stopping when the dough becomes stiff enough to knead. Turn dough onto a lightly floured surface and knead until it's smooth and elastic, about 10 minutes.

2. Place the dough into the greased bowl, turning to coat; then cover with plastic wrap and let it rise until it doubles in bulk, about 1½ hours. Gently punch the dough down; then let it rest for 10 minutes. Shape the dough into 3 loaves; then place them into three greased 9x5-inch loaf pans. Let them rise until just about doubled.

3. Preheat the oven to 350°; then bake until browned and cooked through, 35 to 45 minutes. Invert loaves onto a wire rack to cool; then enjoy a slice warm.

MARTHA WASHINGTON'S POTATO ROLLS

Many recipes are attributed to the nation's first First Lady, but it's unlikely that she was making devil's food cake and chocolate-covered cherries in the 1700s. She was, however, in possession of a manuscript of old family recipes that had been handed down from one generation to the next and eventually came to be published under the name Martha Washington's Book of Cookery and Book of Sweetmeats. *This recipe doesn't appear in that manuscript; still, the name remains, if only to honor a woman who added much to our nation's culinary heritage.*

TOTAL TIME: 4 HOURS • **HANDS-ON TIME:** 1 HOUR • **YIELD:** 4 DOZEN SMALL ROLLS

2	large russet potatoes
¾	cup milk
1	teaspoon table salt
2	tablespoons granulated sugar
3	tablespoons salted butter, plus more for baking sheets
1	package yeast
5–7	cups all-purpose flour
3	tablespoons vegetable oil

1. Peel the potatoes; cut into large chunks. Put potatoes in a medium-size pot and cover with water. Set over high heat and bring to a boil; then reduce heat to a simmer; cook until tender, about 30 minutes. Meanwhile, put milk in a small pan and bring to a simmer over high heat. Remove from heat.

2. When potatoes are tender, drain, reserving the cooking water.

3. Mash the hot potatoes. Add the salt, sugar, and butter and beat well; stir in 1½ cups of the reserved potato water and the hot milk; then cool until lukewarm.

4. Add the yeast and stir in 4 cups of the flour, beating well; then add enough of the remaining flour to make a dough stiff enough to knead (the exact amount will depend on how moist the potato mixture is). Knead on a floured board until smooth and elastic.

5. Brush a large bowl with the vegetable oil; then transfer the dough to the bowl. Turn to coat; then cover and let rise in a warm place until the dough has doubled in bulk, 1½ to 2 hours.

6. Preheat the oven to 400° and grease two large rimmed baking sheets. Punch down the dough and turn it out on a floured board; then pat out to a thickness of about ¾ inch. Divide the dough into 48 portions and shape them into rolls. Arrange on greased pans and let rise until very light and more than doubled in bulk, about 45 minutes. Bake until nicely browned, about 20 minutes. Serve warm.

CONNECTICUT DABS

Here's another variation on the cornmeal cakes first made by Native Americans and then adapted for European tastes. This version is similar to a recipe for "Dodgers, Dabs, or Corn Meal Puffs" from an 1884 cookbook called Mrs. Lincoln's Boston Cook Book: What to Do and What Not to Do in Cooking, *by Mary Johnson Bailey Lincoln. Here, small dabs of dough enriched with sour cream are dropped on a hot baking sheet and baked until golden brown. Serve with soup, chili, or stews, or slather with butter and honey for breakfast.*

TOTAL TIME: 30 MINUTES • HANDS-ON TIME: 15 MINUTES • YIELD: 12 TO 15 DABS

1	cup cornmeal
¾	cup boiling water
1	tablespoon salted butter, softened
1	large egg, lightly beaten
3	tablespoons sour cream
1	tablespoon granulated sugar
½	teaspoon table salt
	Vegetable oil (for baking sheet)

1. Preheat the oven to 450° and place an ungreased baking sheet on the middle rack. Close the door and let the oven and the baking sheet get hot.
2. In a large bowl, beat together the cornmeal and boiling water. Fold in the butter, egg, sour cream, sugar, and salt until just combined. Don't overmix.
3. When the sheet is hot, brush with oil; then drop the batter by spoonfuls onto the sheet and bake until the bottoms are golden brown, about 15 minutes.

MAPLE CORNBREAD

Cornbread is an American adaptation, a necessity food invented by early European settlers who had a shortage of wheat flour and an appetite for bread. Early versions were heavy and dense, but over time, cooks found that adding baking powder and now-plentiful wheat flour produced a bread worth craving. A bit of maple syrup in the mix makes it even more of a treat.

TOTAL TIME: 35 MINUTES • HANDS-ON TIME: 10 MINUTES • YIELD: 9 SQUARES

1⅓	cups all-purpose flour
⅔	cup cornmeal
1	tablespoon baking powder
½	teaspoon table salt
⅔	plus ¼ cup milk
⅓	cup pure maple syrup
¼	cup (½ stick) salted butter, melted, plus more for pan
2	large eggs, slightly beaten

1. Preheat the oven to 425° and grease an 8x8-inch pan or an 8- or 9-inch skillet.
2. In a large bowl, whisk together the dry ingredients; then add the milk, syrup, melted butter, and eggs. Stir until just combined—a few lumps are all right.
3. Pour the batter into the prepared pan or skillet and bake for 25 minutes, or until golden brown and a toothpick inserted into the center comes out clean.

FAN TAN ROLLS
(recipe on opposite page)

FAN TAN ROLLS

These slightly sweet rolls, a.k.a. "New England buttermilk rolls," are the match of any bakery dinner roll. The shaping is easy but looks fancy, and the texture is moist and firm.

TOTAL TIME: 3 HOURS • **HANDS-ON TIME:** 1 HOUR 45 MINUTES • **YIELD:** ABOUT 20 ROLLS

4–5 cups all-purpose flour
⅓ cup granulated sugar
2 teaspoons table salt
½ teaspoon baking soda
2 packages (scant tablespoon each) active dry yeast
1½ cups buttermilk
½ cup salted butter, softened
2 tablespoons salted butter, melted

1. Preheat the oven to 400°. In a large bowl, combine 2 cups flour, sugar, salt, soda, and yeast. Set aside.

2. In a saucepan, heat buttermilk and ½ cup butter until buttermilk is warm (butter doesn't need to melt), around 120°. Add to flour mixture. Blend with mixer at lowest speed until moistened; then beat for 2 minutes at medium speed.

3. By hand, stir in enough of the remaining flour to make a stiff dough. Cover and let rise in a warm place until light and doubled in size (about 1½ hours). Gently deflate dough; then turn onto a floured board. Roll out dough to a 15-inch square, brush with 2 tablespoons of melted butter, and cut dough into 1½-inch-wide strips. Stack 5 strips together and cut into stacks 1½ inches long. Repeat with remaining strips. Place 1 stack cut side down into each greased muffin cup.

4. Cover and let rise until doubled (about 30 minutes). Bake 15 to 18 minutes, or until golden brown. Serve warm.

ENGLISH MUFFIN BREAD

Yankee's senior lifestyle editor, Amy Traverso, got this recipe from a friend's mother, Sue Williams, who always had loaves of delicious homemade bread on hand to toast for breakfast. Because you let it rise only once, with a generous amount of yeast, it develops the rough texture of English muffins, with their signature nooks and crannies, and a wonderfully crisp crust.

TOTAL TIME: 1 HOUR 30 MINUTES · **HANDS-ON TIME:** 25 MINUTES · **YIELD:** 2 LOAVES

Butter (for pans)
2 tablespoons cornmeal
5¾ cups all-purpose flour, divided
2 packages (scant tablespoon each) active dry yeast
1 tablespoon granulated sugar
2 teaspoons table salt
¼ teaspoon baking soda
2 cups milk
½ cup water

1. Grease bottoms and sides of two 9x5-inch loaf pans and sprinkle with cornmeal; tilt and shake the pans to coat evenly.
2. In a large bowl, combine 3 cups flour with the yeast, sugar, salt, and baking soda. Combine milk and water and heat until quite warm (120° to 130°). Add to the dry ingredients and beat well. Add the remaining flour, about 1 cup at a time, and stir until smooth. Divide the dough among the two prepared pans.
3. Cover the loaves with a kitchen towel and set in a warm spot to rise for 40 minutes. Fifteen minutes before you're ready to bake the loaves, preheat the oven to 400°. Then bake until nicely browned, 25 to 30 minutes.

MONKEY BREAD

The first recipes for "monkey bread," a sweet pull-apart bread glazed with a rich caramel sauce, appeared in American cookbooks in the 1940s, but there are 19th-century recipes for breads made from little balls of dough baked together in the same pan. Most contemporary recipes for monkey bread start with store-bought dough, but nothing beats homemade biscuits, and they're very quick and easy to put together.

TOTAL TIME: 1 HOUR 15 MINUTES • **HANDS ON TIME:** 40 MINUTES • **YIELD:** ABOUT 10 SERVINGS

FOR THE BISCUIT DOUGH:

- 1 **cup plus 1 tablespoon granulated sugar, divided**
- 2 **teaspoons ground cinnamon**
- ½ **cup buttermilk**
- 1 **large egg**
- 3 **cups all-purpose flour, plus more for dusting**
- 2½ **teaspoons baking powder**
- 1½ **teaspoons kosher or sea salt**
- ½ **teaspoon baking soda**
- 8 **tablespoons cold unsalted butter, cut into small cubes, plus more for pan**
- ½ **cup chopped walnuts (optional)**

FOR THE SAUCE:

- 6 **tablespoons salted butter, melted**
- 1 **cup firmly packed light-brown sugar**

1. Lightly dust a large piece of parchment paper with flour and set aside. Pour 1 cup sugar and the cinnamon into a large zip-top bag; seal, shake, and set aside. Butter a standard 9-inch tube or Bundt pan and set aside.

2. Make the dough: In a small bowl, whisk together the buttermilk and egg; set aside. In a medium-size bowl, whisk together the flour, remaining 1 tablespoon sugar, baking powder, salt, and baking soda. Sprinkle the butter over the flour mixture and use your fingers to work it in. (Rub your thumb against your fingertips, smearing the butter as you do; see p. 181, bottom.) Stop when the mixture looks like sand studded with little chunks.

3. Add the egg mixture and stir with a fork just until the dough begins to hold together. It will look quite ragged and not fully blended, but stop there. You want to prevent the butter from melting into the dough; those little chunks will create a flakier texture once baked.

4. Preheat the oven to 350° and set a rack to the middle position. Dump the dough out onto the prepared piece of parchment paper and knead *just* enough to bring it all together into a ball. Use your hands to press the dough out on the parchment to a 1-inch thickness. Cut the biscuits into 1½-inch pieces. Put the pieces, about 8 at a time, into the bag with the cinnamon/sugar mix. Toss to coat, then arrange them in the prepared pan. If using walnuts, arrange them in and among the biscuit pieces as you go. Repeat the process with the remaining biscuit dough.

5. Make the sauce: In a small saucepan over medium-high heat, melt the salted butter with the brown sugar; then bring to a boil. Boil for 1 minute; then pour over the biscuits. Transfer the pan to the oven and bake until firm and golden brown, about 35 minutes. Let the bread cool in the pan for 10 minutes; then turn out onto a plate. To serve, pull the bread apart with your fingers—no need to use a knife!

CHEDDAR–SCALLION BEER BREAD

With its raw ingredients of grain and yeast, beer is sometimes referred to as "liquid bread," so it makes sense that you can, in fact, make bread with beer. The brew adds flavor and helps the bread rise, making this one of the easiest loaves you'll ever prepare: no kneading, no rising time. You'll need an additional leavening agent in the form of baking powder, and we also added cheddar cheese and scallions for extra flavor.

TOTAL TIME: 50 MINUTES • **HANDS-ON TIME:** 10 MINUTES • **YIELD:** 1 LOAF

Salted butter (for pan)
2 cups all-purpose flour
1 cup whole-wheat flour
1 cup finely grated sharp cheddar cheese
3 scallions (green onions), white parts removed, sliced very thinly crosswise
1½ tablespoons granulated sugar
1 tablespoon baking powder
1 teaspoon table salt
1 12-ounce bottle dark ale or hearty beer, at room temperature
3 tablespoons salted butter, melted

1. Preheat the oven to 375°. Grease a 9x5-inch bread pan and set aside. In a mixing bowl, stir together the flours, cheese, scallions, sugar, baking powder, and salt. Add the beer all at once, mixing only until just combined; the batter should be lumpy.

2. Pour the batter into the prepared pan and drizzle with melted butter. Bake until the top is golden brown and a toothpick inserted into the center comes out clean, 35 to 40 minutes. Turn out onto a rack to cool. Serve warm.

HOMEMADE GRAHAM CRACKERS

Sylvester Graham of Northampton, Massachusetts, was a 19th-century health reformer who advocated a bland vegetarian diet of whole grains, fresh fruits, and vegetables. He did invent a cracker made with his signature whole-wheat flour blend, but it was virtually unsweetened and bore only a glancing resemblance to these delicious treats.

When making these crispy homemade graham crackers, the magic word is "chill." Frequent trips to the fridge during the shaping and cutting process will keep the sticky dough cold enough to handle. Make traditional large crackers or use cookie cutters for fun shapes. The size of the cookies and thickness of the dough will dictate how long they need to bake, so keep a close eye!

TOTAL TIME: 3 HOURS 45 MINUTES • **HANDS-ON TIME:** 1 HOUR • **YIELD:** 10 CRACKERS

- **3 cups unbleached all-purpose flour,** plus more for work surface
- **1 cup dark-brown sugar, lightly packed**
- **1 teaspoon baking soda**
- **¾ teaspoon kosher salt**
- **½ cup (1 stick) unsalted butter, very cold,** cut into 1-inch cubes
- **⅓ cup mild-flavored honey (such as clover)**
- **5 tablespoons whole milk**
- **2 tablespoons vanilla extract**
- **3 tablespoons granulated sugar**
- **1 teaspoon ground cinnamon**

1. In a food processor or the bowl of a standing mixer with paddle attachment, thoroughly combine flour, brown sugar, baking soda, and salt. Add butter and pulse or mix on low, until mixture is the consistency of coarse meal.

2. In a small bowl, whisk together honey, milk, and vanilla. Add to flour/butter mixture. Pulse on and off a few times, or mix on low until dough barely comes together. (It will be soft and sticky.) Turn dough out onto a floured work surface and shape into a 1-inch-thick rectangle. Wrap in plastic and chill until firm, about 2 hours, or overnight.

3. In a small bowl, combine sugar and cinnamon, and set aside. Divide dough in half and return one half to the refrigerator. On a floured work surface, shape dough into a long rectangle about ⅛ inch thick. (Dough may be a bit sticky, so flour as necessary or roll between two sheets of floured parchment or plastic wrap.) Trim rectangle so that it's about 4 inches wide and 18 inches long; then cut into four 4x4½-inch pieces. Gather scraps and set aside.

4. Place dough pieces on parchment-lined baking sheets and sprinkle with cinnamon/sugar mixture. Chill until firm, about 30 minutes.

5. Repeat with remaining dough. Gather all scraps into a ball and chill until firm. Dust work surface with flour and roll out dough for 2 to 3 more crackers.

6. Preheat the oven to 350°. Mark a vertical line down the middle of each cracker, without cutting through dough. Using a toothpick or skewer, prick dough in 2 rows to mimic the look of a commercial graham cracker.

7. Bake 25 minutes, until browned and slightly firm to the touch, rotating sheets halfway through to ensure even baking.

POPOVERS

Popovers are an American invention, the offspring of British batter puddings. According to John Mariani's Encyclopedia of American Food and Drink, *"settlers from Maine who founded Portland, Oregon, Americanized the pudding from Yorkshire by cooking the batter in custard cups lubricated with drippings from the roasting beef (or sometimes pork) . . . The result is called Portland popover pudding, individual balloons of crusty meat-flavored pastry."*

While it isn't required, a popover pan's deep, separated cups yield taller, grander results than its muffin-pan counterpart. To let the steam do its "pop" job, resist the temptation to open the oven at any time during baking, and you'll be deliciously rewarded.

TOTAL TIME: 50 MINUTES · **HANDS-ON TIME:** 15 MINUTES · **YIELD:** 6 LARGE OR 12 SMALL POPOVERS

1 **cup whole milk**
3 **large eggs, beaten**
2 **tablespoons salted butter, melted,**
    plus more for pan and for serving
1 **teaspoon kosher or sea salt**
1 **cup all-purpose flour**
    Jam (for serving)

1. Preheat the oven to 450°. Grease the cups of a popover or muffin pan and place on the lowest rack of the oven.
2. In a large bowl, whisk together the milk, eggs, 2 tablespoons butter, and salt. Add the flour and whisk vigorously until smooth and frothy.
3. Pour batter into the preheated pan, filling each cup slightly more than halfway. Bake 20 minutes; then reduce heat to 350° and bake an additional 15 to 20 minutes, or until tops are deep golden brown. Check their progress through the oven window; don't open the oven door until popovers are done.
4. Remove from the oven and pierce each popover with a knife to let steam escape. Serve piping hot with butter and jam.

PARKER HOUSE ROLLS

Boston's Parker House hotel is indeed the source of these delightfully soft and puffy dinner rolls, which were invented around the 1870s. Tales of its origin vary, but most center around a beleaguered chef who, in a fit of pique, threw some unfinished rolls into the oven and found that they turned out even better than his usual recipe.

TOTAL TIME: 3 HOURS 30 MINUTES • **HANDS-ON TIME:** 45 MINUTES • **YIELD:** 2 DOZEN

1½ **cups milk**
5½ **cups all-purpose flour, divided,
       plus more for work surface**
⅓ **cup granulated sugar**
2 **teaspoons table salt**
1 **package (scant tablespoon) active dry yeast**
¾ **cup (1½ sticks) salted butter, softened, divided,
       plus more for bowl**
1 **large egg**

1. Grease a large bowl and set aside. In a small saucepan, heat the milk until warm, but not hot (120°).

2. In a large bowl (or the bowl of a standing mixer with paddle attachment), combine 2½ cups flour, sugar, salt, and yeast. Add ½ cup (1 stick) of the butter and beat well. With your mixer on low speed, gradually add the warm milk to the dry ingredients.

3. Add the egg and increase mixer speed to medium. Beat for 2 minutes, occasionally scraping the bowl with a rubber spatula. Gradually add in the remaining 3 cups flour, until the dough is tacky but not sticky. If you're using a standing mixer, switch to the dough hook when the dough starts to get stiff.

4. Knead the dough until smooth and elastic, about 10 minutes by hand, or 5 minutes if you're using a mixer. Shape the dough into a ball and place in the prepared bowl, flipping the dough to grease the top. Cover with a clean towel and let it rise in a warm place until doubled in size, about 1½ hours.

5. Gently deflate the dough and turn onto a lightly floured surface. Knead lightly to make a smooth ball, and then cover for 15 minutes to let the dough rest.

6. Line two baking sheets with parchment and preheat the oven to 375°.

7. In a small saucepan, melt the remaining ¼ cup butter.

8. On a lightly floured surface with a floured rolling pin, gently roll dough out to a ½-inch thickness. Using a 2½- to 3-inch round biscuit cutter dipped in flour, cut dough into circles.

9. Holding each dough circle by the edge, brush both sides with the melted butter. Lay each dough circle onto a baking sheet; then fold in half, pressing the edge to seal it shut.

10. Arrange folded dough circles in rows, each nearly touching the next. Cover with a towel and let the rolls rise in a warm place until nearly doubled in size, about 40 minutes.

11. Bake for 20 minutes, or until golden brown.

CRANBERRY–ORANGE STACK CAKE
(recipe on page 148)

Desserts and Sweets

When we searched Yankee's archives for the foods that would fill this book, it became clear that the pie, cake, cookie, pastry, and candy recipes in our trove were the most timeless of the lot and the easiest to adapt to contemporary tastes. Fads may come and go, but sweets never truly go away—they're too delicious to be lost. Stack cakes, apple dumplings, lemon meringue pie, cream puffs, popcorn balls, and thumbprint cookies are as appealing today as they were in our grandmothers' day.

AUNT MAE'S THUMBPRINT COOKIES

About 20 years ago, we ran this recipe with a story from reader Charlotte S. Undercoffer: "My mother died when I was 13, and my father's sister tried to make Christmas special for me and my brother. The most important day during the holiday season was the day that we baked Aunt Mae's thumbprint cookies. After we had mixed all the ingredients, she put the little balls of dough on the baking pan. Then we used our thumbs to make the indentation for the jelly. (It always had to be cherry jelly for us—but any kind is good.)"

TOTAL TIME: 1 HOUR 30 MINUTES • HANDS-ON TIME: 45 MINUTES • YIELD: 16 COOKIES

- ½ **cup (1 stick) salted butter, softened**
- ¼ **cup firmly packed light-brown sugar**
- 1 **large egg, separated**
- 1 **cup all-purpose flour**
- 1 **teaspoon vanilla extract**
- ½ **teaspoon table salt**
- 1 **cup chopped walnuts**
- ½ **cup cherry, raspberry, or strawberry jam, divided**

1. In the bowl of a standing mixer or, if using a hand-held mixer, in a large bowl, beat butter and brown sugar until light and fluffy, about 4 minutes. Add egg yolk, flour, vanilla, and salt, and mix well.

2. Preheat the oven to 400°. In a small bowl, beat the egg white until frothy. Put walnuts in another small bowl.

3. Roll cookie dough into walnut-size balls; then roll each ball in the egg white and then the walnuts. Arrange on two ungreased cookie sheets and press the center of each cookie with your thumb (this is a great activity for young kids). Bake 5 minutes; then reduce heat to 325°. Bake 8 minutes more; then remove the cookies from the oven and check to see whether the thumbprints remain. If not (the cookies do tend to puff up), use the handle of a wooden spoon to re-press the thumbprints; then return the cookies to the oven until they're light golden brown, 5 to 7 more minutes. Remove from oven and cool at least 30 minutes; then spoon a bit of jam into the center of each cookie.

**AUNT MAE'S THUMBPRINT COOKIES,
BLACK & WHITES**
(recipes opposite and on page 114)

BLACK & WHITES

New Yorkers may claim these cookies as their own, but anyone who grew up in New England with a decent bakery nearby probably has deep memories of these tender cookies with the chocolate and vanilla icings on top.

This recipe ran in the June 1999 issue of Yankee. *Reader Helen Beatty Beal wrote, "During the hard-time 1930s, our family of seven lived in Boston. Papa was lucky to keep a low-paying job, and Mama made all our clothes, baked our bread, and planned each meal to stretch Papa's pay. We always had nourishing but dull desserts, such as bread or rice pudding, gingerbread, or applesauce.*

"Our summers were spent in a small cottage on Hough's Neck, Quincy. The cottage had minimal cooking facilities, and desserts were eliminated except for very special occasions. I was sent to the Laurel Crest Bakery with 35¢ to purchase seven 'Black-and-Whites.' I'll never forget how good these shop-baked goodies tasted, and I always associate them with special happenings and our wonderful, carefree summers."

TOTAL TIME: 1 HOUR • **HANDS-ON TIME:** 45 MINUTES • **YIELD:** ABOUT 2 DOZEN 4-INCH COOKIES

NOTE: *Frosting the cookies while they are still slightly warm makes it much easier to spread the glazes.*

FOR THE COOKIES:
- 3 cups all-purpose flour
- 1 teaspoon baking powder
- 1 teaspoon baking soda
- ½ teaspoon table salt
- ½ cup vegetable shortening,
    plus more for baking sheets
- ¼ cup salted butter
- 1½ cups granulated sugar
- 2 large eggs
- 1 teaspoon vanilla extract
- 1 cup buttermilk
    (or 1 cup milk plus 2 teaspoons vinegar)

FOR THE CHOCOLATE GLAZE:
- 4 tablespoons cocoa powder (Dutch-process or natural)
- 3 tablespoons plus 1 teaspoon warm water
- 2 tablespoons vegetable oil
- 2 tablespoons light corn syrup
- 2 cups confectioners' sugar

FOR THE VANILLA GLAZE:
- 2 cups confectioners' sugar
- 2 tablespoons warm water
- 1 tablespoon light corn syrup
- ½ teaspoon vanilla extract

1. Preheat the oven to 375° and grease two baking sheets (or line with parchment paper). Set aside.
2. First, make the cookies: In a medium-size bowl, whisk together the flour, baking powder, baking soda, and salt, and set aside. In a large bowl, cream the shortening, butter, and sugar together until light and fluffy, about 4 minutes. Add the eggs and 1 teaspoon vanilla and beat well. Add one-third of the flour mixture and mix briefly; then add one-third of the buttermilk and mix again. Repeat twice until all ingredients are fully combined.
3. Drop the cookie batter by the tablespoon onto the prepared baking sheets, leaving about 2 inches between cookies. Bake until golden brown at the edges, 12 to 15 minutes, rotating pans halfway through the baking.

(recipe continues on next page)

4. Meanwhile, make the glazes: For the chocolate, stir the cocoa, water, oil, and corn syrup together in a small saucepan over low heat. Whisk in confectioners' sugar and beat until smooth. Set aside.

5. For the vanilla glaze, stir together the confectioners' sugar, water, corn syrup, and vanilla until smooth.

6. When the cookies are done, transfer to wire racks to cool. While they're still slightly warm (see "Note," opposite), use a small off-set spatula to frost half of each cookie with the vanilla glaze. Let them dry for 5 minutes; then rinse the spatula and apply the chocolate glaze to the other halves.

MARY'S LEMON–NUTMEG MELTAWAYS

Bliss! A light, lemony cookie that's a snap to make. Cornstarch makes it truly melt-in-your-mouth tender, and the lemon–nutmeg flavor is bright and unexpected. It'll be a welcome addition to your holiday-cookie repertoire.

TOTAL TIME: 40 MINUTES • HANDS-ON TIME: 20 MINUTES • YIELD: ABOUT 3 DOZEN COOKIES

1 ¼ **cups cake flour**
¼ **cup cornstarch**
¼ **teaspoon table salt**
10 **tablespoons unsalted butter, softened**
½ **teaspoon freshly grated nutmeg**
½ **cup confectioners' sugar, plus more for glass**
2 **tablespoons fresh lemon juice**
1 **tablespoon freshly grated lemon zest**

1. Preheat the oven to 325°. Sift cake flour, cornstarch, and salt onto waxed paper.

2. Beat the rest of the ingredients in the mixer until light and fluffy. Add dry ingredients and beat on low speed until mixture is smooth.

3. Shape teaspoonfuls of dough into balls and place on ungreased baking sheets. Using the bottom of a glass dipped in confectioners' sugar, flatten balls slightly into 1¼-inch circles.

4. Bake until golden brown around the edges, 15 to 17 minutes. Cool on baking sheets for 2 minutes; then transfer to wire racks to finish cooling.

GRANDMA TAILOR'S SUGAR COOKIES

We love the story of this recipe's origins, which came from a reader named Diane Elliott: "My grandmother, Agnes Tailor, was famous in the little Iowa town where she lived (and in her family) for her wonderful sugar cookies. Although I've never known for sure, I suspect the recipe may have come in the covered wagon when her parents, Eliza Ann and Carleton Braley, went from Vermont to Iowa in about 1860. Certainly Grandma never had a written recipe, always making the cookies from memory. When I was a teenager in the 1940s, my mother finally was able to get Grandma to write the recipe out and send it to us.

"Well, we tried that recipe several times and the cookies were okay, but not melt-in-your-mouth good like Grandma's. She insisted it was just our imagination, however, because 'That's exactly the way I make them.' Finally... when it was time to replenish her cookie supply, Mother sat and watched. Grandma talked as she stirred the cookie dough, reciting the recipe: 'One cup shortening,' she said, and in the bowl went the (aha!) one cup of real butter. 'Two eggs, beaten,' went in the bowl. Then Grandma said, 'A half-cup of milk,' and into the bowl went (aha again!) a half-cup of heavy cream. At last we knew why hers were so much better than ours!"

TOTAL TIME: 1 HOUR 15 MINUTES • **HANDS-ON TIME:** 30 MINUTES • **YIELD:** 5 TO 6 DOZEN COOKIES, DEPENDING ON SIZE

1½ **cups granulated sugar**
1 **cup salted butter, softened,**
   plus more for baking sheets
2 **large eggs**
½ **cup heavy cream**
1 **teaspoon vanilla extract**
4 **cups all-purpose flour, plus more for work surface**
1½ **teaspoons baking powder**
½ **teaspoon table salt**

1. Using a handheld or standing mixer, cream sugar and butter until light and fluffy, about 4 minutes. Add eggs, one at a time, stirring well after each. Beat in cream and vanilla. Add flour, baking powder, and salt, and stir. Turn dough out onto a piece of waxed paper, press into a disk, and refrigerate at least 30 minutes (up to 3 days).

2. Preheat the oven to 350°. Grease 2 baking sheets or line with parchment paper and set aside.

3. On a lightly floured counter, roll the dough out to a ⅛-inch thickness, and cut into shapes using a cookie cutter. Gather and roll the dough again as needed. Transfer the cookies to the prepared sheets and bake until golden brown, 12 to 15 minutes.

JOE FROGGERS

Molasses–spice cookies date back to the Colonial era, but this variation with rum in the batter comes from Marblehead, Massachusetts. Locals say the cookies are named after Joseph Brown, a free African American man who served in the Revolutionary War and opened a tavern in town. His wife, Lucretia Brown, did the cooking, and these cookies, made in an iron skillet, were her specialty. According to Marblehead Myths, Legends, and Lore *by Pam Matthias Peterson, "when the batter hit the pan, it ran in all directions and formed shapes that looked like a frog's body and legs." (Our recipe produces a firm dough rather than batter.) Given their shape and the fact that the tavern was next to a frog pond, the name stuck.*

TOTAL TIME: 50 MINUTES PLUS 45 MINUTES CHILLING • **HANDS-ON TIME:** 40 MINUTES • **YIELD:** 4 DOZEN COOKIES

- ⅓ **cup plus 1 tablespoon hot water**
- 2½ **tablespoons dark rum, such as Gosling's**
- 3–3½ **cups all-purpose flour, plus more for work surface**
- 1½ **teaspoons table salt**
- 1 **teaspoon baking soda**
- 1¼ **teaspoons ground ginger**
- ½ **teaspoon ground cloves**
- ½ **teaspoon ground allspice**
- ¼ **teaspoon freshly grated nutmeg**
- ½ **cup (1 stick) salted butter, softened, plus more for baking sheets**
- 1 **cup granulated sugar**
- 1 **cup unsulphured dark molasses**

1. In a small bowl, combine hot water and rum. In a large second bowl, whisk together 3 cups flour with the salt, baking soda, and spices. Set aside.

2. In another large bowl, cream together butter and sugar until light and fluffy, about 4 minutes.

3. Add water and rum to creamed mixture and beat well. Add one-third of the flour mixture and stir; then stir in half the molasses, scraping down the sides as you go. Repeat with an additional third of the flour mixture and the remaining molasses. Finally, add the rest of the flour mixture. If dough seems too loose, add the extra ½ cup flour.

4. Divide the dough into two balls, cover with plastic wrap, and chill at least 45 minutes (up to overnight).

5. Preheat the oven to 375° and grease two baking sheets or line with parchment.

6. You have two options for shaping the cookies: On a floured surface, you can roll the dough out to a ½-inch thickness and use a floured 2-inch cookie cutter or drinking glass to cut the dough into rounds. Transfer the cookies to the prepared baking sheets, leaving about 2 inches between cookies. Or you can skip the rolling and instead break off walnut-size pieces of dough and roll them into balls between your palms. Arrange the balls on the baking sheets. Put some granulated sugar into a bowl and press the bottom of a drinking glass into the sugar; then press it onto each ball of dough, flattening it before baking.

7. Bake the cookies until set but still soft in the middle, about 10 minutes. Cool on wire racks.

YANKEE'S CRISP-CHEWY WAFFLE IRON BROWNIES

This recipe first ran in a 1953 issue of Yankee, *appearing in a story called "Recipes from Old 'Receipt' Books" by Nancy Dixon. It begins, "One of the nicest things that happens to us in the* Yankee *Recipe Department is when we receive really and truly fascinating cookbooks that also serve a worthy cause. Our latest acquisition is* Two Hundred Years of Lebanon Valley Cookery . . . *The book—with a scrubbed white cover with an easy-to-handle blue spiral binding—is by the Ladies Guild Church of Our Savior (Episcopal) in Lebanon Springs, N.Y., and the cookery editor has rightfully starred some of the following as unusual, ancient, and modern." This recipe is so clever that we're wondering why it ever got lost. The waffle iron gives the brownies crispy ridges, but the inside remains rich and fudgy. They're novel and fun and incredibly easy to make.*

TOTAL TIME: 35 MINUTES · HANDS-ON TIME: 35 MINUTES · YIELD: 10 TO 12 BROWNIES

NOTE: *You need to let the brownies sit for a minute on the hot, opened iron before trying to remove them. Otherwise they'll be too soft and likely to crumble.*

- ½ **cup salted butter, softened**
- 1¼ **cups granulated sugar**
- 3 **squares unsweetened (baking) chocolate, melted**
- 1 **teaspoon vanilla extract**
- 2 **large eggs, beaten**
- 1⅓ **cups all-purpose flour**
- ½ **teaspoon baking powder**
- ½ **teaspoon table salt**
  Vegetable oil (for waffle iron)
  Garnish: powdered sugar

1. Preheat your waffle iron. In the bowl of a standing mixer, cream butter and sugar until fluffy. Add melted chocolate and vanilla and stir. Add eggs, one at a time, stirring well after each.
2. In a separate bowl, whisk together flour, baking powder, and salt. Add dry ingredients to chocolate mixture and stir just until evenly combined.
3. When the waffle iron is ready, spray or brush with vegetable oil. Drop a heaping tablespoonful of batter into the center of each grid on your iron. Close the lid and cook until the brownies are crisp and dry on the outside, 4 to 6 minutes, depending on the iron (check after 4 minutes). Open the waffle iron and let brownies sit for 1 to 2 minutes, until firm enough to remove (don't skip this step). Transfer to a plate and sprinkle with powdered sugar. Repeat with remaining batter.

**YANKEE'S CRISP-CHEWY
WAFFLE IRON BROWNIES**
(recipe on opposite page)

SOUR CREAM "MONKEY FACE" COOKIES

Mildred Starratt Robbins grew up in Boston, but spent summers with her grandparents on their Nova Scotia farm. In 1996, she wrote to us to share her grandmother's best cookie recipe and tell the story of its origin. "The place was pure joy to me when I was a child," she wrote. "Cottage Cove, Nova Scotia, nestled against the temperamental Bay of Fundy, was a village of eight houses, a wharf, a fish house, a smokehouse, and an assortment of barns, cool icehouses, woodsheds, carriage sheds, and outhouses. Every year we took the SS Yarmouth or Evangeline out of Boston late on a summer afternoon and arrived in Yarmouth the next morning. Off we went to the eight-room farmhouse where my grandparents raised nine children without benefit of electricity, running water, or central heat.

"The kitchen was everyone's favorite room, and the big old stove was in use every day. My brother and I were happy to search the shoreline for kindling wood in hopes that Grandma would make cookies. Sometimes cream would sour since there was no refrigeration . . . and then Grandma would make Monkey Face Cookies. Decorating the soft cookies with three raisins for eyes and mouth was often my job."

These delicious morsels taste like sugar cookies with a bit more tang, and though Mildred liked to decorate her with raisins, we also recommend chocolate chips.

TOTAL TIME: 35 MINUTES · **HANDS-ON TIME:** 25 MINUTES · **YIELD:** ABOUT 3 DOZEN COOKIES

4 **tablespoons (½ stick) salted butter, softened, plus more for cookie sheets**
1 **cup granulated sugar**
1 **large egg, lightly beaten**
½ **cup sour cream**
1 **teaspoon vanilla extract**
2 **cups plus 2 tablespoons all-purpose flour**
1 **teaspoon baking soda**
¼ **teaspoon table salt**
   Garnish: raisins or chocolate chips

1. Preheat the oven to 350°. Grease two cookie sheets (or line with parchment paper) and set aside. Combine butter and sugar in a medium-size bowl and beat with a handheld or standing mixer until light and fluffy, about 4 minutes. Add egg and beat; then add sour cream and vanilla and mix well. In a separate bowl, whisk together the flour, baking soda, and salt; then add to the wet mixture and stir just until evenly combined.

2. Drop batter, a teaspoon at a time, onto the prepared cookie sheets. Arrange 3 raisins or chocolate chips on each to make a face (2 eyes and a dot for a mouth). Transfer to the oven and bake until golden brown, 8 to 10 minutes.

MAIDS OF HONOR TARTS

According to British cooking maven Delia Smith, these tarts are rumored to have originated at Richmond Palace in the 16th century. The fillings have changed over the years—ours are made with jam and a simple almond-paste topping—but the appeal of these bite-size treats hasn't changed at all.

TOTAL TIME: 1 HOUR 30 MINUTES • HANDS-ON TIME: 45 MINTES • YIELD: ABOUT 42 TARTS

NOTE: *Almond flour is available at many supermarkets these days—look for it in the gluten-free or natural-foods aisle (Bob's Red Mill is a popular brand). You can also find it at natural-foods stores, Whole Foods markets, or gourmet shops. You may substitute hazelnut flour or pistachio flour, if you prefer.*

FOR THE CRUST:

- 2½ cups all-purpose flour, plus more for work surface
- ⅓ cup granulated sugar
- ½ teaspoon table salt
- 1 cup (2 sticks) chilled unsalted butter, plus more for pans
- 6–8 tablespoons ice water
  Confectioners' sugar (for dusting)

FOR THE FILLING:

- 1 large egg
- ½ cup granulated sugar
- ⅔ cup almond flour (see "Note," above)
- 1½ tablespoons milk
- ½ teaspoon almond extract
- ¼ teaspoon table salt
- ¾ cup seedless raspberry or strawberry jam

1. First, make the crust: In a medium-size bowl, whisk together the flour, sugar, and salt. Add the butter to the bowl and use a pastry cutter or a fork to break it down into small pieces. Next, use your fingers to work the butter into the flour. (Rub your thumb against your fingertips, smearing the butter as you do.) Stop when the mixture looks like cornmeal with some pea-sized bits of butter remaining (see p. 181). Sprinkle 6 tablespoons of ice water over the mixture and stir with a fork until the dough begins to come together. If needed, add 1 or 2 more tablespoons of water.

2. Turn the dough out onto a lightly floured counter and knead three times, or just enough to make a cohesive dough. Gather the dough into a ball, then divide into two pieces. Press each piece into a disk and wrap in plastic wrap. Refrigerate for at least 20 minutes.

3. Meanwhile, make the filling. Using a mixer, beat together the egg and sugar for 1 minute. Add the almond flour, milk, almond extract, and salt, and beat until combined. Set aside.

4. Preheat the oven to 400° and set an oven rack to the bottom position. Grease the cups of 2 mini-muffin pans (or line with paper liners) and set aside.

5. Remove the first disk of dough from the refrigerator, dust the counter with more flour, and roll the dough out to a ¼-inch thickness, turning it often to prevent sticking. Cut the dough into rounds using a 2½- to 3-inch-wide biscuit cutter or drinking glass. Gather and roll the dough again as needed to use up scraps.

6. Tuck a pastry round into each of the muffin cups, folding the dough as needed to make it fit. Spoon a scant teaspoonful of jam into each of the tarts and top with a spoonful of the almond topping.

7. Repeat with remaining dough, jam, and topping. Transfer to the oven and bake until nicely browned on top, 18 to 22 minutes. Garnish with a dusting of confectioners' sugar.

LEMON SHERBET
(recipe on opposite page)

LEMON SHERBET

The word sherbet *comes from the Arabic* sharab *or* sharbat, *a cold, sweetened drink usually made with fruit juice. Over time, the cold fruit juices were frozen into fruit desserts. Sherbets probably reached their peak of popularity in this country from the 1950s to the 1970s when Howard Johnson's orange sherbet was its signature dessert. Today, sorbets, made with only fruit and sugar, are more popular, whereas sherbets, which contain a small amount of milk or cream, are less common.*

But this dessert—submitted by reader Irmarie Jones, who received it from her mother-in-law in the 1950s—will hopefully reintroduce you to sherbet. It manages to be simultaneously rich, creamy, zingy, and light, all while taking less than 15 minutes to prepare. Given the amount of cream in the recipe, it probably qualifies as more of an ice cream than a sherbet, but its texture is lighter. Really, it's in a class of its own.

TOTAL TIME: 3 HOURS • **HANDS-ON TIME:** 15 MINUTES • **YIELD:** ABOUT 1 QUART (8 SERVINGS)

NOTE: *You can make this recipe by simply freezing the mixture in a glass or plastic container, but you'll get the smoothest texture if you prepare it in an ice cream maker.*

Juice of 2 large lemons
1½ **cups granulated sugar**
1½ **cups milk**
1 **cup heavy cream**

1. In a medium-size bowl, whisk together the lemon juice and sugar until sugar is mostly dissolved. Add the milk and whisk until sugar is fully dissolved. In a separate bowl, whip the cream to medium peaks.

2. Gently fold the whipped cream into the lemon mixture and transfer to an ice-cream maker or an airtight freezer-safe container (see "Note," left). Freeze according to manufacturer's instructions. For firmer sherbet, transfer to your freezer for at least 2 hours before serving.

RASPBERRIES ROMANOFF

Despite all the tensions between the United States and the Soviet Union in the middle of the 20th century, classic Russian fare, such as beef Stroganoff, caviar, and raspberries Romanoff, was considered the height of sophistication. This simple dessert remains a great way to serve an elegant parfait that you can prepare between courses.

TOTAL TIME: 8 MINUTES • HANDS-ON TIME: 8 MINUTES • YIELD: 6 SERVINGS

2 **cups vanilla ice cream, softened**
1 **cup heavy cream, whipped**
¼ **cup no-pulp orange juice**
2 **quarts raspberries, fresh or frozen and thawed**
½ **cup confectioners' sugar**

1. Place softened ice cream and whipped cream in a bowl and beat with a fork until blended. Stir in orange juice.
2. Meanwhile, crush berries in medium-size bowl and stir in confectioners' sugar.
3. Spoon into glasses or dessert cups, alternating cream and berry mixtures. Serve immediately.

RHUBARB PUDDING

Everything comes up rosy in this pudding, which proves that rhubarb doesn't need strawberries to shine.

TOTAL TIME: 1 HOUR • HANDS-ON TIME: 15 MINUTES • YIELD: 6 TO 8 SERVINGS

4 **cups chopped rhubarb (¾-inch chunks)**
1 **cup plus ½ cup granulated sugar**
¼ **cup unsalted butter, melted, plus more for baking dish**
1 **teaspoon vanilla extract**
2 **large eggs, well beaten**
½ **cup all-purpose flour**
½ **cup whole-wheat flour**
1 **teaspoon baking powder**
½ **teaspoon table salt**

1. Preheat the oven to 375° and butter a 2-quart baking dish.
2. In a large mixing bowl, toss together the rhubarb and 1 cup of the sugar.
3. In a medium-size bowl, combine the melted butter, vanilla, eggs, both flours, baking powder, the remaining ½ cup of sugar, and salt.
4. Add rhubarb to the batter and stir to combine. Pour the batter into the prepared baking dish. Transfer to the oven and bake until the pudding is browned on top but still a bit soft inside, about 45 minutes.

CHESTNUT CREAM

This recipe was a 1959 contribution by a reader named Mrs. Pauline McConnell, who wrote, "I wish someone would revive the chestnut dishes of long ago. We always had baskets of chestnuts in our root cellar at home. One of our favorite dishes was chestnut cream. This dish is approximately 150 years old and has been passed down from generation to generation in my family."

TOTAL TIME: 40 MINUTES • **HANDS-ON TIME:** 10 MINUTES • **YIELD:** 6 SERVINGS

NOTE: *Using preroasted, vacuum-packed chestnuts sold in glass jars saves time and makes this recipe easy. Look for them in supermarkets during the holidays and in most gourmet and Whole Foods stores year-round (a warning, though: they can be expensive off-season). Don't use the canned type, which generally lack flavor. To roast chestnuts yourself, cut an X through the flat bottom of each nut (this helps with peeling later). Toss chestnuts with ⅓ cup of canola oil. Spread on a baking sheet and roast at 425° until tender, 25 to 35 minutes. Return chestnuts to the bowl, toss, and cover bowl with plastic wrap. Cool, then peel.*

1½ **pounds peeled, roasted chestnuts, roughly chopped (see "Note," above)**
1½ **cups milk**
1 **cup granulated sugar**
1 **cup water**
1 **teaspoon vanilla extract**
1 **cup heavy cream, whipped to firm peaks**
Garnish: chocolate shavings

1. In a small saucepan over medium-high heat, simmer chestnuts with milk until soft, about 10 minutes. In a small saucepan, combine the sugar and water and simmer until the sugar dissolves.
2. Drain chestnuts, discarding milk, and purée in a food processor with sugar syrup until smooth. Transfer to a medium-size bowl and chill in the refrigerator until cool, 30 minutes. When cool, stir in the vanilla and fold in the whipped cream. Pile into a dish and chill before serving. Garnish with chocolate curls if you like.

GRAPE-NUT PUDDING

America went mad for breakfast cereals in the late 1800s, when the Kellogg brothers founded the Battle Creek Sanitarium and the Sanitas Food Company, advocating a diet rich in whole grains. Rival cereal maker C. W. Post, a former patient at Battle Creek, created "Grape-Nuts" in 1897. The pudding came soon after. We found a recipe for Grape-Nut pudding in a 1901 church cookbook published by the Dudley Street Baptist Church in Boston, and the dish appears to have gained wider national popularity by the 1920s. It seems that New Englanders have a particular fondness for this creamy custard with its cereal "crust" on the bottom, and many of our great diners still feature it on their menus.

TOTAL TIME: 1 HOUR 30 MINUTES • **HANDS-ON TIME:** 25 MINUTES • **YIELD:** 8 SERVINGS

Butter (for baking dish)
4 cups milk
1 cup Grape-Nuts cereal
4 large eggs
½ cup (scant) granulated sugar
2½ teaspoons vanilla extract
¼ teaspoon table salt
½ teaspoon freshly grated nutmeg
Garnish: whipped cream (optional)

1. Preheat the oven to 350° and butter a 2-quart baking dish. Put milk and Grape-Nuts in a medium-size saucepan over medium-high heat and bring to a simmer. Remove from heat, stir, and let cool 15 minutes. In a medium-size bowl, beat eggs with sugar, vanilla, and salt. Add the cooled milk and Grape-Nuts to egg mixture and stir well. Pour into the prepared baking dish. Sprinkle nutmeg over the top. Set the baking dish into a deep roasting pan.

2. Place in the oven and pour water into the roasting pan, enough to reach halfway up the side of the baking dish. Bake until almost set in the center, 50 to 60 minutes. There should be a very slight jiggle when you shake the pan, and a knife inserted into the center should come out clean. Let the pudding set on top of the stove for at least 20 minutes before serving. Serve plain or with whipped cream.

POPPY'S RICE PUDDING

We love it when readers send us their family recipes, especially when there are stories attached. Jim Juliano sent us this one in 1998, along with the story of his grandfather, James Anastasio, who immigrated to America from Italy in 1904, at the age of 12. "He settled in the New Haven, Connecticut, area and soon began working in the restaurant business," Jim wrote. "By 1920, he opened up the Sterling Restaurant on State Street. In 1949 . . . he opened the J.A. Restaurant a few blocks away on Temple Street. There he remained until his retirement in the late 1950s.

"After his retirement, Sunday 'dinner' (an early afternoon event) at Poppy's became a family tradition, with my grandfather and his wife, Margie, surrounded by their five children and eight grandchildren. The meal often included pot roast or chicken pot pie and a lively discussion of the events of the day. Dessert was likely Poppy's famous rice pudding."

We love how this recipe bakes into a two-layer treat: silky custard on top, with tender rice and raisins underneath. If you prefer, you can also make this pudding in a double boiler on the stovetop. Just be sure to keep the water at a simmer so the eggs don't curdle.

TOTAL TIME: 1 HOUR 20 MINUTES • **HANDS-ON TIME:** 30 MINUTES • **YIELD:** 6 TO 8 SERVINGS

Butter (for baking dish)
4 **extra-large eggs**
⅔ **cup granulated sugar**
¼ **teaspoon table salt**
1 **teaspoon vanilla extract**
4 **cups milk**
1 **cup cooked rice**
½ **cup raisins (optional)**
Garnish: ground cinnamon

1. Butter a 9x13-inch baking dish. Set aside. Bring a kettle of water to a simmer. Preheat the oven to 325°.
2. In a large mixing bowl, beat the eggs well. Beat in sugar, salt, vanilla, and milk; then add rice and raisins (if using). Pour into the prepared baking dish and sprinkle the top with cinnamon.
3. Place the filled dish into a larger pan; then fill that pan with the simmering water so that it comes about halfway up the outside of the baking dish. Bake until custard is just firm and lightly browned on top, 45 to 60 minutes.

BAKED CRANBERRY PUDDING

This pudding is loosely based on a recipe we received about 20 years ago from reader Debra Arnold-Codd. Her grandmother, "Gram Howard," always served a steamed cranberry pudding at Thanksgiving: "Gramp always gets the first piece. I'm not sure if the pudding is the highlight of our Thanksgiving or if it's watching Gramp enjoy it!" This version, baked in an oven rather than steamed, takes much less time than Gram Howard's, but it's still served with a delicious butter sauce, a nod to traditional English puddings.

TOTAL TIME: 1 HOUR • HANDS-ON TIME: 20 MINUTES • YIELD: 6 TO 8 SERVINGS

FOR THE PUDDING:

- 2 cups all-purpose flour
- 1 cup granulated sugar
- 2½ teaspoons baking powder
- ¼ teaspoon table salt
- 3 tablespoons salted butter, melted, plus more for the pan
- ⅔ cup milk
- 1 large egg
- 1½ cups finely chopped fresh cranberries

FOR THE SAUCE:

- 8 tablespoons (1 stick) salted butter
- 1 cup granulated sugar
- ⅔ cup light cream
- ¼ teaspoon vanilla extract

1. Preheat the oven to 350° and grease an 8-inch square baking pan. Make the pudding: In a large mixing bowl, whisk together the dry ingredients. Add butter, milk, and egg, and beat for 2 minutes. Stir in the cranberries. Pour mixture into the prepared pan. Bake until nicely browned and set in the middle, 40 to 45 minutes.

2. Meanwhile, make the sauce: In a small saucepan, melt the butter over low heat. Add sugar and cream and cook, stirring, over medium heat, until sauce is smooth. Remove from heat and stir in vanilla. Spoon warm sauce over individual servings.

INDIAN PUDDING

Early colonists brought with them to America a fondness for British "hasty pudding," a dish made by boiling wheat flour in water or milk until it thickened into porridge. Since wheat flour was scarce in the New World, settlers adapted by using native cornmeal, dubbed "Indian flour," and flavoring the resulting mush to be either sweet (with maple syrup or molasses) or savory (with drippings or salted meat). In time, the dish evolved into one that was resoundingly sweet, with lots of molasses and additional ingredients such as butter, cinnamon, ginger, eggs, and sometimes raisins or nuts. Recipes for Indian pudding began appearing in cookery books in the late 1700s.

TOTAL TIME: 2 HOURS 30 MINUTES • **HANDS-ON TIME:** 30 MINUTES • **YIELD:** 6 TO 8 SERVINGS

4 **cups whole milk**
½ **cup cornmeal**
½ **cup molasses**
¼ **cup maple syrup (any grade)**
2 **tablespoons unsalted butter, softened, plus more for baking dish**
2 **large eggs, beaten**
1 **teaspoon table salt**
2 **teaspoons granulated sugar**
½ **teaspoon ground cinnamon**
½ **teaspoon ground ginger**
⅛ **teaspoon freshly grated nutmeg**
Garnish: vanilla ice cream or whipped cream (optional)

1. Preheat the oven to 300° and grease a 1½-quart baking dish.
2. Bring milk to a simmer in a double boiler over high heat. Slowly add the cornmeal, whisking to combine. Continue to cook, whisking often, for 15 minutes.
3. Add molasses slowly; then remove from heat. Add maple syrup and the rest of the ingredients, and stir until smooth.
4. Pour mixture into the prepared baking dish, and bake until the pudding is set and the top is browned, about 2 hours. Serve hot or cold, topped with vanilla ice cream or whipped cream.

DR. BOYLSTON'S HONEYCOMB PUDDING

If you've ever traveled down Boylston Street in Boston, you may have wondered where the street got its name. It pays honor to Dr. Zabdiel Boylston, who braved the threat of mob violence in 1721 in order to get Bostonians inoculated against smallpox. In doing so, he introduced vaccination to the United States. Boylston also performed the first surgery by an American physician and removed the first breast tumor in 1718. He was also the great-uncle of President John Adams.

This pudding, which tastes a bit like a very moist gingerbread topped with lemon sauce, was one of his favorite desserts. As it cooks, the baking soda bubbles, leaving the little holes from which the dish gets its name.

TOTAL TIME: 45 MINUTES • HANDS-ON TIME: 30 MINUTES • YIELD: 8 SERVINGS

FOR THE PUDDING:

- ½ **cup all-purpose flour, plus more for pan**
- ½ **cup granulated sugar**
- ½ **teaspoon ground cinnamon**
- ¼ **teaspoon ground cloves**
- ¼ **teaspoon ground allspice**
- ¼ **teaspoon table salt**
- ½ **cup (1 stick) salted butter, melted, plus more for pan**
- ½ **cup warm milk**
- 4 **large eggs, beaten**
- 2 **teaspoons baking soda**
- ¾ **cup molasses**

FOR THE SAUCE:

- 1 **cup granulated sugar**
- ¼ **cup (½ stick) salted butter, softened**
- **Juice of 1 lemon**
- 1 **large egg, beaten**
- ¼ **teaspoon table salt**
- 3 **teaspoons cornstarch**
- 1 **cup simmering water**

1. Preheat the oven to 350°. Butter and flour a 9x5-inch loaf pan and set aside.
2. Make the pudding: In a large bowl, whisk together the flour, sugar, spices, and salt. Add the melted butter, milk, eggs, baking soda, and molasses, and stir to combine. Pour the mixture into the prepared pan and bake until firm, 30 to 40 minutes.
3. Meanwhile, make the sauce: Working off the heat, put the sugar and butter in a medium-size saucepan and stir. Add the lemon juice, egg, salt, and cornstarch, and stir. Add the simmering water; then set the pot over low heat and cook, stirring continuously, until the mixture thickens.
4. When the pudding is cooked, turn it out on a warmed serving dish. Slice (the honeycomb will show); then spoon the sauce over the slices and serve warm.

BLACKBERRY COBBLER

"We lived in the country," wrote reader Dorry Lou Wharton about this family recipe, which she sent to us in the early 1990s, "and every summer Mother would take me blackberry picking . . . We would fill our buckets with sweet berries and head for home, where Mother always made us a delicious blackberry cobbler. I look back on those times with such fond memories, and I have passed the recipe on to my own daughters . . . I had my husband plant [blackberry bushes] in our garden. Today as I fill my pail and walk across the lawn, my mouth starts to water thinking of the blackberry cobbler I will soon be making."

TOTAL TIME: 55 MINUTES · **HANDS-ON TIME:** 15 MINUTES · **YIELD:** 6 SERVINGS

¼ **cup salted butter, softened, plus more for pan**

⅔ **plus ¼ cup granulated sugar, divided**

1 **cup all-purpose flour**

2 **teaspoons baking powder**

¼ **teaspoon table salt**

½ **cup milk**

2–2½ **cups blackberries**

1 **cup pomegranate, cherry, or berry juice**

Ice cream (optional)

1. Grease an 8-inch square baking pan. Preheat the oven to 375° and set a rack to the middle position.
2. In the bowl of a standing mixer or, if using a hand-held mixer, in a large bowl, beat together butter and ⅔ cup sugar for 2 minutes. In a medium-size bowl, whisk together flour, baking powder, and salt. Add dry ingredients to butter mixture and stir to combine. Add milk and beat until smooth. Pour into baking pan. Sprinkle with blackberries; then pour the juice over all and sprinkle with remaining ¼ cup sugar. Bake until golden brown, 35 to 45 minutes. Serve warm with ice cream, if you'd like.

ORCHARD FRUIT SLUMP
(recipe on opposite page)

ORCHARD FRUIT SLUMP

A "slump" is a fruit dessert made in a skillet and topped with sweet biscuits. It's a variation on "cobbler" (which is often cooked in a baking dish). Meanwhile, a "grunt" is a slump prepared in a covered pot on the stove so that the steam cooks the biscuits.

TOTAL TIME: 55 MINUTES • **HANDS-ON TIME:** 35 MINUTES • **YIELD:** 6 TO 8 SERVINGS

NOTE: *You can substitute any fruit, as long as the total volume is 6 cups. If your fruit is particularly juicy, reduce the water by ½ cup.*

FOR THE FILLING:

- 3 cups peaches, peeled, cut into ½-inch wedges (see "Note," above)
- 1½ cups cherry halves
- 1½ cups plums, cut into ½-inch wedges
- ⅔ cup firmly packed light-brown sugar
- ¼ cup all-purpose flour
- 1½ tablespoons fresh lemon juice
- ½ teaspoon ground ginger

FOR THE TOPPING:

- 1½ cups all-purpose flour
- ½ cup quick-cooking oats
- 1 tablespoon baking powder
- ½ teaspoon ground cinnamon
- ⅓ cup granulated sugar
- 1 large egg, slightly beaten
- ⅓ cup mik
- ⅓ cup salted butter, melted
- Cinnamon sugar

1. Preheat the oven to 400°. Toss fruit with brown sugar, flour, juice, and ginger. Pour into a 10- to 12-inch cast-iron pan. Put in oven for about 15 minutes.
2. Meanwhile, make the biscuit dough: In a large bowl, whisk together flour, oats, baking powder, cinnamon, and sugar. Add beaten egg, milk, and melted butter, stirring just until moist. Don't overmix.
3. Remove fruit from oven and drop dough onto fruit, forming about 8 mounds. Sprinkle with cinnamon sugar. Bake until biscuits are lightly browned and juices are bubbling, 15 to 20 minutes.

SUMMER BERRY TRIFLE WITH CORNMEAL CAKE

This simple recipe comes from the kitchens of Sterling College in Vermont, where chef Anne Obelnicki and her team source most of their ingredients from Sterling's own farm and others in the Northeast Kingdom. It's beautiful arranged in a single 8- or 9-inch glass trifle bowl or in individual serving glasses, and it's so delicious you'll want to make trifle a regular part of your dessert repertoire. Feel free to use any combination of raspberries, blueberries, currants, and/or gooseberries.

TOTAL TIME: 2 HOURS 30 MINUTES · HANDS-ON TIME: 45 MINUTES · YIELD: 12 SERVINGS

FOR THE CAKE AND TRIFLE:
- 1 stick (8 tablespoons) plus 5 tablespoons unsalted butter, softened, plus more for pan
- 1 cup granulated sugar
- 2 large eggs
- 1 teaspoon vanilla extract
- ½ cup plain yogurt, whole or low-fat
- 1 cup all-purpose flour, plus more for pan
- ⅔ cup yellow or blue cornmeal
- 1 teaspoon baking powder
- ¼ teaspoon baking soda
- 6 cups fresh raspberries
- ½ cup honey

FOR THE WHIPPED CREAM:
- 3 cups heavy cream
- 2 tablespoons honey

1. Preheat the oven to 350°. Butter and flour a 9x5-inch loaf pan. With a standing or handheld mixer, cream butter and sugar until smooth and light, about 4 minutes. Add eggs and vanilla and beat to combine. Add yogurt and blend.

2. In a separate bowl, whisk together flour, cornmeal, baking powder, and baking soda. Add dry ingredients to the wet ingredients and mix well. Spoon batter into the prepared pan and bake until a toothpick inserted into the center comes out with moist crumbs attached but no wet batter, about 1 hour.

Cool completely on a rack, about 45 minutes. You may make the cake a day in advance.

3. Reserve 1 cup of the prettiest raspberries and place the rest of the berries in a bowl; add the honey, folding gently just to combine. Set the mixture aside to macerate for 10 minutes.

4. Make the whipped cream: Put heavy cream in a chilled bowl and beat until very loose peaks form. Add honey and continue beating until medium peaks form. Set aside.

5. To assemble the trifle, cut cornmeal pound cake into ½-inch-thick slices. Line bottom of a 9-inch glass bowl with slices of cake, breaking pieces as necessary to fill in the gaps. Spoon half the berry mixture over the cake, being sure to spoon the juices evenly. Cover with half the whipped cream, spreading to the edge. Repeat with another layer of cake, berries, and cream. Sprinkle the reserved whole raspberries over the top layer of whipped cream.

6. Serve right away or refrigerate, covered, for up to two hours.

BUTTERMILK BLUEBERRY BUCKLE

By definition, a "buckle" is a cake studded with fruit and capped with a crumble topping. The berries settle down into the cake batter during cooking, while most of the pecan-crumble mixture stays on top. Buttermilk lends a delicate tang.

TOTAL TIME: 1 HOUR 10 MINUTES • **HANDS-ON TIME:** 35 MINUTES • **YIELD:** 10 SERVINGS

NOTE: *If you don't have buttermilk on hand, you can substitute clabbered milk: Add 1 tablespoon of lemon juice or white wine vinegar to 1 cup of whole or 2% milk and let stand for 10 minutes before using.*

FOR THE TOPPING:

- 1 **pound fresh or frozen blueberries**
- ¼ **teaspoon plus 1 teaspoon ground cinnamon**
- 1 **tablespoon granulated sugar**
- ½ **cup firmly packed light-brown sugar**
- ⅓ **cup all-purpose flour**
- ¼ **teaspoon freshly grated nutmeg**
- ½ **cup finely chopped pecans**
- 3 **tablespoons cold salted butter, cut into small cubes, plus more for pan**

FOR THE CAKE:

- 7 **tablespoons salted butter, at room temperature**
- ¾ **granulated sugar**
- 2¼ **cups all-purpose flour**
- 1½ **teaspoons baking powder**
- ½ **teaspoon baking soda**
- 1½ **teaspoons kosher or sea salt**
- 1 **cup buttermilk (see "Note," above)**
- 1 **large egg**

1. Preheat the oven to 350°. Grease a 9x13-inch baking pan. In a medium-size bowl, toss the blueberries with the ¼ teaspoon cinnamon and 1 tablespoon sugar. Set aside.

2. Meanwhile, in a small bowl, toss the remaining 1 teaspoon cinnamon with the brown sugar, flour, nutmeg, and pecans. Scatter the cold butter over all, and use a pastry cutter or fork to work it in until the mixture looks like very lumpy wet sand. Refrigerate until ready to use.

3. Make the cake: Using a standing or handheld mixer with a whisk attachment, cream together the butter and sugar in a large bowl until the mixture is fluffy and very pale, 5 to 8 minutes. In a separate bowl, whisk together the flour, baking powder, baking soda, and salt. In a third bowl, whisk together the buttermilk and egg. Add one-third of the flour mixture to the butter mixture. Mix briefly; then add half the buttermilk/egg blend and mix again. Repeat, then finish with the remaining flour mixture and stir just until combined.

4. Spread the batter evenly into the baking pan (it will be quite thick). Sprinkle blueberries over the batter; then sprinkle the crumble topping over all.

5. Bake until the top is golden and a toothpick inserted into the center comes out clean, 35 to 45 minutes. Let cool on a rack for 30 minutes; then serve warm from the pan.

CREAM PUFFS

The choux pastry that forms the shell for these custard-filled delights dates back several hundred years, and cream-filled puffs have been around at least since the days of Antoine Carême, the famous 18th-century French pastry chef. But here in America, many people associate cream puffs with dessert buffets of the 1950s and 1960s. (Choux pastry puffs were also commonly stuffed with savory fillings, such as chicken or egg salad.)

TOTAL TIME: 2 HOURS 30 MINUTES • **HANDS-ON TIME:** 1 HOUR 30 MINUTES • **YIELD:** 24 TO 34 CREAM PUFFS

FOR THE PUFFS:

- 2 sticks (1 cup) salted butter
- 2 cups water
- 2 cups all-purpose flour
- ½ teaspoon table salt
- 8 large eggs

FOR THE FILLING:

- ¾ cups granulated sugar
- ¼ cup cornstarch
- 2 large eggs
- ¼ teaspoon table salt
- 2 cups milk
- 2 tablespoons salted butter
- ½ cup heavy cream, whipped to firm peaks
- 1 teaspoon vanilla extract
  Garnish: powdered sugar

1. Preheat the oven to 425° and set a rack to the middle position. Line 2 baking sheets with parchment paper.
2. Put butter and water in a medium-size saucepan on high heat and bring to a simmer. Add flour and salt all at once, and stir until mixture forms a smooth ball. Remove from heat. Transfer dough to a bowl and add the eggs, one at a time, mixing well after each addition.
3. Spoon or pipe balls tablespoon-size balls of dough onto the prepared baking sheets, leaving 2 inches between them. Transfer to the oven and cook until the puffs are golden, 25 to 30 minutes. (Don't open the oven door; look through the window instead.) Reduce heat to 350° and bake until nicely browned, about 15 minutes. Remove from oven and cut a small slit into the side of each puff to let the steam out. Transfer to a wire rack to cool.
4. Meanwhile, make the filling: In a medium-size bowl whisk together sugar, cornstarch, eggs, and salt. Put the milk and butter in a small pot over medium-high heat and bring to a simmer. Remove from heat. Drizzle ½ cup of the hot milk mixture into the egg mixture, whisking continuously (see p. 181, top). Repeat with an additional ½ cup hot milk. Pour this egg mixture back into the pot with the milk and increase heat to medium-high. Cook, stirring often, until mixture begins to bubble and thicken. Transfer to a bowl, cover with plastic wrap pressed against the surface, and cool in the refrigerator at least 1 hour (up to overnight).
5. When ready to use, whip the cream with the vanilla until it forms firm peaks. Fold into the cold custard. Use a pastry bag fitted with a metal tip to fill each cream puff or simply slice puffs in half and fill with cream. Sprinkle with powdered sugar and serve.

**PAVLOVA WITH FRESH STRAWBERRIES
& WHIPPED CREAM**
(recipe on opposite page)

PAVLOVA WITH FRESH STRAWBERRIES & WHIPPED CREAM

Australians and New Zealanders have an ongoing debate about who first created this gorgeous meringue dessert crowned with whipped cream and fresh fruit. You may substitute other berries, kiwi, or mango, but we love it best with strawberries.

TOTAL TIME: 3 HOURS • **HANDS-ON TIME:** 45 MINUTES • **YIELD:** 8 SERVINGS

FOR THE MERINGUE:
- 4 large egg whites
- ⅛ teaspoon table salt
- 1 cup granulated sugar
- 1 teaspoon vanilla extract
- 1 teaspoon white or cider vinegar
- 2 teaspoons cornstarch

FOR THE TOPPING:
- 1 pint (about 12 ounces) fresh strawberries
- ¼ cup granulated sugar
- 1 tablespoon freshly squeezed lemon juice

FOR THE WHIPPED CREAM:
- 1½ cups heavy cream
- 1 tablespoon granulated sugar
- 1½ teaspoons vanilla extract

1. Preheat the oven to 300°. Line a sheet pan with parchment paper, trace a 9-inch circle in the center (we used a cake pan as our guide), and turn the paper over.

2. In the clean bowl of a standing mixer with a whisk attachment, beat egg whites until frothy. Add salt and continue beating. As soft peaks form, slowly add sugar in a thin stream, beating as you go. Once sugar is incorporated, beat on high speed until firm, shiny peaks begin to form, about 2 more minutes. Stop beating; then gently fold in vanilla, vinegar, and cornstarch with a spatula.

3. Spoon the meringue into the center of the traced circle and use the back of the spoon to spread it out to the edges, creating a shallow well in the middle. Put into the oven, reduce heat to 250°, and bake 1½ hours. Turn off the oven, leaving meringue inside until it turns crisp and pale but is still a bit soft inside, about 1 hour. Remove from oven and let cool completely.

4. While meringue bakes, prepare the fruit: Hull and slice or quarter the berries (depending on size). Mix gently with sugar and lemon juice in a medium-size bowl. Set aside.

5. Whip cream, sugar, and vanilla with an electric mixer or whisk until firm peaks form. To serve, carefully peel parchment from meringue and place gently on a large serving platter. Spread whipped cream over meringue. Spoon berries over the top and serve.

APPLE DUMPLINGS

Apple dumplings have roots in Pennsylvania Greman country, where the pastries emerged as a clever use for leftover pie dough on baking day. They're so delicious, though, that we're happy to make up a fresh batch of pastry just for these alone. The sauce thickens as it cooks, turning into a rich and glossy syrup.

TOTAL TIME: 1 HOUR 30 MINUTES • HANDS-ON TIME: 50 MINUTES • YIELD: 6 DUMPLINGS

FOR THE DOUGH:
- **2 cups all-purpose flour**
- **2 teaspoons baking powder**
- **½ teaspoon table salt**
- **1 tablespoon granulated sugar**
- **6 tablespoons cold unsalted butter, cut into small cubes**
- **2 tablespoons cold vegetable shortening**
- **½ cup cold milk**

FOR THE SAUCE:
- **1 ¾ cups fresh apple cider**
- **½ cup dark rum, such as Gosling's**
- **½ cup firmly packed light-brown sugar**

FOR THE APPLES:
- **¼ cup firmly packed light-brown sugar**
- **½ teaspoon ground cinnamon**
- **6 small firm-sweet apples, such as Pink Lady, Jonagold, or Gala (about 4 ounces each or 1 ½ pounds total)**

1. Cut two pieces of parchment paper so they're 11 inches wide and 16 inches long. Set aside.
2. Make the dough: In a medium-size bowl, whisk together flour, baking powder, salt, and sugar. Sprinkle the butter cubes and shortening on top and use your fingers to work them into the dough. Stop when the mixture resembles cornmeal with some pea-sized pieces of butter remaining (see p. 181, bottom). Add milk and stir, using a fork, until dough begins to hold together.
3. Turn the dough out onto one of the pieces of parchment paper; knead three times, or until the dough feels cohesive. Shape dough into a rough rectangle and cover with the second piece of parchment paper. Roll dough out to roughly the same size as the parchment paper. Carefully transfer to refrigerator; let chill for 30 minutes.
4. Preheat the oven to 425°. Meanwhile, make the sauce: In a medium-size saucepan heat cider, rum, and brown sugar over high heat. Bring to a simmer and cook for 5 minutes. Remove from heat and set aside.
5. Prepare the apples: In a small bowl, stir together brown sugar and cinnamon; set aside. Peel and core apples; trim if necessary to make each about 3 inches tall.
6. Remove the dough from the refrigerator and remove the top layer of parchment. Use a ruler and a knife to trim the dough to an exact 10x15-inch rectangle. Cut dough into six 5-inch squares. Set one apple in the center of each square; fill centers of apples with brown-sugar mixture. Bring corners of dough up together around apples to make four points, gently sealing at top and along seams so that the pastry fits snugly.
7. Place dumplings in a large baking dish. Pour sauce around dumplings and transfer to oven; bake for 10 minutes. Reduce oven temperature to 375° and bake until dumplings are golden brown and sauce is bubbling, 25 to 30 minutes more. Serve warm in bowls with extra sauce.

APPLE DUMPLINGS
(recipe on opposite page)

**MARBLE BUNDT CAKE
WITH CHOCOLATE GLAZE**
(recipe on opposite page)

MARBLE BUNDT CAKE WITH CHOCOLATE GLAZE

From 1966 to 1994, Sylvia Hocking of Thomaston, Maine, ran a small home-based bakery that brought her national fame for her coffee cake, blueberry muffins, raspberry buckle, and strawberry pie. She later published a cookbook, Sylvia's Cakes & Breads: Famous Recipes from a Small Maine Kitchen *(Down East Books, 1998). We published a handful of her recipes in our March 1995 issue, and this cake, moist and rich with chocolate swirls, reminds us of the beauty of old-fashioned Bundts.*

TOTAL TIME: 2 HOURS 30 MINUTES • HANDS-ON TIME: 45 MINUTES • YIELD: 10 SERVINGS

FOR THE CAKE:
- 2¾ cups all-purpose flour
- 2¼ teaspoons baking powder
- 1 teaspoon table salt
- 1 cup (2 sticks) unsalted butter, softened, plus more for pan
- 1¾ cups granulated sugar
- 1 teaspoon vanilla extract
- 4 extra-large eggs
- ¾ cup milk
- 4 ounces bittersweet chocolate, melted
- ¼ teaspoon baking soda

FOR THE GLAZE:
- 2 squares (2 ounces) unsweetened baking chocolate
- 3 tablespoons unsalted butter
- 1½ cups confectioners' sugar
- 3–4 tablespoons hot water
- 1 teaspoon vanilla extract

1. Preheat the oven to 350°. Grease a 10-inch Bundt or tube pan. Whisk together the flour, baking powder, and salt. Set aside.
2. In the bowl of a standing mixer or, if using a hand-held mixer, in a large mixing bowl, cream the butter and sugar until light and fluffy, 3 to 4 minutes. Add vanilla and mix; then add eggs one at a time, mixing well after each. Add one-third of the dry ingredients, then half the milk. Repeat, scraping down the bowl periodically. Add the remaining third of the dry ingredients and mix until combined.
3. Divide the batter into two bowls. Add the melted chocolate and baking soda to one of the bowls and stir until evenly combined.
4. To make the marble effect, drop the batters into the prepared pan by the heaping tablespoon, alternating between chocolate and vanilla batches. Try to distribute the batter evenly around the pan.
5. Once all of both batters are in the pan, bang it several times on the counter to make the batter level. Use a thin knife to swirl through the mixture several times.
6. Bake until a cake tester comes out clean and the cake is fragrant, 60 to 75 minutes. Run a knife around the edges, unmold onto a wire rack, and let cool completely.
7. While cake is cooling, make the glaze: Melt the chocolate with the butter in a small saucepan or in the microwave. Add the confectioners' sugar, hot water, and vanilla at the same time and whisk until smooth. If the glaze seems too thick, add a bit more water. If it's too thin, add some more sugar.
8. When cake is cool, set the rack over a baking sheet or cutting board. While the glaze is still warm, pour it evenly over the cake, letting it drip down the sides and onto the sheet. Let the cake sit 5 minutes before serving.

FLOURLESS (GLUTEN-FREE) CHOCOLATE CREAM ROLL

"This recipe was a favorite when I was growing up," writes Mrs. J.F. Bradley, who shared it with us some years back. *"My mom made it often, and regularly she would make one for Dad at work. Dad was a dentist, and his office was in a building with an adjoining dental laboratory. Now my two youngest daughters request it for dessert for Christmas dinner!"*

We love this cake as is—especially because it makes such a delicious dessert for people who can't tolerate gluten—but here's a fun variation: Double the whipped cream and fold in ½ cup finely crushed peppermint candy, omitting the sugar and vanilla. Roll half the cream inside the cake and use the remainder to frost.

TOTAL TIME: 1 HOUR 20 MINUTES • **HANDS-ON TIME:** 1 HOUR • **YIELD:** 10 SERVINGS

Butter (for pan)
Flour (for pan and parchment)
5 large eggs, at room temperature
Pinch table salt
1 cup confectioners' sugar
5 tablespoons cocoa powder (natural or Dutch-process),
plus more for dusting
½ pint heavy cream, whipped and mixed with
1 teaspoon vanilla and 2 tablespoons sugar

1. Preheat the oven to 350° and set a rack to the middle position. Grease the bottom, but not the sides, of a 15½ x10½ x1-inch baking pan (a jellyroll-size pan). Line with parchment paper and make sure to leave a flap at both ends to help you lift the cake out of the pan when done.

2. Separate the eggs. Using a standing mixer and a very clean bowl, beat the egg whites with the salt until firm peaks form. Transfer to another bowl and set aside. Beat the egg yolks for 1 minute, until creamy; then add the sugar. Beat for an additional minute. Add the cocoa and beat thoroughly.

3. Fold ¼ of the beaten whites into the chocolate mixture to lighten it; then gently fold in the remainder in 2 batches. Pour this mixture into the prepared jellyroll pan and smooth the top.

4. Bake until the cake feels springy to the touch and a cake tester comes out clean, about 15 minutes. Turn out at once onto a tea towel dusted with cocoa powder. Remove the parchment paper; turn the cake so that it's oriented vertically and roll up from the bottom, rolling the towel in as you go. Let cool completely; then gently unroll and spread with the sweetened whipped cream. Roll again and chill before slicing.

COFFEE CLOUD SPONGE CAKE

Sponge cakes are a late-18th/early-19th-century creation, achieving a light texture through beating egg yolks and sugar together until they turn pale and lemon-colored. This recipe also uses beaten egg whites and baking powder, so it achieves beautifully lofty heights, as the name implies. The mild coffee flavor is enhanced by the satiny icing.

TOTAL TIME: 2 HOURS 30 MINUTES • **HANDS-ON TIME:** 45 MINUTES • **YIELD:** 10 SERVINGS

FOR THE CAKE:

- 1 tablespoon instant coffee grounds
- 1 cup boiling water
- 2 cups sifted all-purpose flour
- 1 tablespoon baking powder
- ½ teaspoon table salt
- 6 eggs, separated
- ½ teaspoon cream of tartar
- ½ cup plus 1½ cups granulated sugar
- 1 teaspoon vanilla extract
- 1 cup finely chopped pecans or walnuts

FOR THE ICING:

- 2 tablespoons salted butter, softened
- 2 cups confectioners' sugar
- 1½ teaspoons instant coffee grounds
- ¼ teaspoon table salt
- 2–3 tablespoons milk
  Garnish: chopped pecans or walnuts (optional)

1. Preheat the oven to 350°. In a small bowl, dissolve instant coffee in boiling water, and set aside to cool.
2. In a medium-size bowl, whisk together flour, baking powder, and salt.
3. In a large bowl, beat egg whites with cream of tartar until soft peaks form. Add ½ cup of the sugar to the egg whites a little at a time, and continue beating until firm, glossy peaks form. Set whites aside.
4. In another large mixing bowl, beat egg yolks until smooth; then gradually add remaining 1½ cups sugar and vanilla. Beat at high speed until thick and lemon-colored (about 5 minutes).
5. Add the dry ingredients alternately with the cooled coffee to the egg-yolk mixture, beginning and ending with dry ingredients. Blend thoroughly. Fold in nuts. Lightly fold in the beaten egg whites until evenly blended.
6. Pour into an ungreased 10-inch tube pan and bake until fully cooked, 60 to 70 minutes.
7. Immediately invert the pan and set the hole in the center atop a heatproof funnel or bottle to let it cool upside-down (this protects the cake from sinking). Cool completely, about 45 minutes.
8. Meanwhile, make the icing: Cream butter; then add confectioners' sugar, instant coffee, and salt, and mix well. Gradually add milk until icing is of spreading consistency. Frost the cake and sprinkle with chopped nuts if you like.

PUMPKIN CREAM CHEESE ROLL
(recipe on opposite page)

PUMPKIN CREAM CHEESE ROLL

If rolling up a cake intimidates you, don't roll from the short end, but rather from the long side of the baked cake. That way, you'll have fewer turns to make—and fewer chances for the cake to crack or tear. This autumn-hued log can be served year-round but is particularly suited for the Thanksgiving table.

TOTAL TIME: 1 HOUR 50 MINUTES • **HANDS-ON TIME:** 35 MINUTES • **YIELD:** 10 SERVINGS

NOTE: *The nuts may go inside the roll or decorate the outside; the choice is yours when you roll the cake.*

- **3** large eggs
- **1** cup granulated sugar
- **⅔** cup canned pumpkin purée (not pie filling)
- **¾** cup all-purpose flour, plus more for paper
- **½** teaspoon ground cinnamon
- **1** teaspoon baking soda
- **½** cup finely chopped walnuts or thinly sliced almonds
- **¾** cup confectioners' sugar, plus more for dusting towel and garnish
- **1** teaspoon maple syrup (any grade)
- **½** teaspoon vanilla extract
- **2** tablespoons unsalted butter, softened, plus more for pan and paper
- **10** ounces whipped cream cheese

1. Preheat the oven to 375°. Grease the bottom, but not the sides, of a 15½ x10½ x1-inch baking pan (a jelly-roll-size pan). Line with baking parchment paper and make sure to leave a flap at both ends to help you lift the cake out of the pan when done. Grease and lightly flour the parchment paper.

2. In a large bowl, beat the eggs on high for 5 minutes. Gradually add the granulated sugar, then the pumpkin. Beat in the flour, cinnamon, and baking soda.

3. Spread the batter evenly across the pan. Sprinkle the nuts over the batter (see "Note," above left).

4. Bake until the batter is set and the cake feels springy to the touch, 14 to 15 minutes.

5. Place a clean linen or cotton dish towel larger than the baking pan on a countertop or other flat surface. Dust it with confectioners' sugar.

6. Immediately turn the cake out onto the dish towel, using mitts and grasping the flaps of parchment. Peel off the parchment paper. Starting at the long side, roll up the cake in the towel, making sure to curl in—not merely fold—the cake during the first roll. Let the cake cool in the towel completely.

7. To make the filling, beat the confectioners' sugar, maple syrup, vanilla, and butter in a medium-size mixing bowl until well blended. Beat in the cream cheese until smooth.

8. When the cake is cool, carefully unroll it. Spread the cream-cheese filling to within an inch of the edges. Roll the cake again. Cover the cake and refrigerate for at least 1 hour or until ready to serve. Dust with additional confectioners' sugar.

CRANBERRY–ORANGE STACK CAKE

In 19th-century Appalachia, a stack cake served as a potluck wedding cake, as members of the community would contribute layers. It's easy to make, since the dough resembles that of giant sugar cookies.

TOTAL TIME: 2½ HOURS PLUS AT LEAST 24 HOURS CHILLING · **HANDS-ON TIME:** 1 HOUR 30 MINUTES · **YIELD:** 12 SERVINGS

NOTE: *This cake has six layers, each baked individually. If you have a large oven and a big pan collection, you can bake them all at once. Otherwise, the recipe is based on the assumption that you'll be using three.*

FOR THE FILLING:
- 4 cups fresh or frozen cranberries
- 1¼ cups granulated sugar
- ¾ cup fresh orange juice
- 1½ teaspoons freshly grated orange zest

FOR THE CAKE:
- 1 cup granulated sugar
- ¾ cup firmly packed light-brown sugar
- 16 tablespoons (2 sticks) unsalted butter, softened, plus more for pans
- 5½ cups all-purpose flour, plus more for work surface and pans
- 2 teaspoons baking powder
- 1½ teaspoons baking soda
- 1 teaspoon table salt
- 1 teaspoon ground cinnamon
- ⅔ cup buttermilk
- 2 extra-large eggs
- 1 tablespoon vanilla extract
- Garnish: confectioners' sugar

1. First, make the filling: In a 4-quart pot over high heat, combine cranberries, sugar, orange juice, and orange zest. Cover and bring to a boil; then reduce heat to medium-low. Simmer, stirring often, until cranberries soften, split their skins, and sauce thickens a bit, 10 to 15 minutes. Purée with a blender until smooth and creamy. Mixture should have the texture of ketchup. If it's too thick, add a few more tablespoons orange juice. Set aside, or cover and refrigerate up to 5 days.

2. Butter and flour cake pans (see "Note," left). In the bowl of a standing mixer (or using a handheld mixer), cream sugars and butter together at medium speed until quite fluffy, 3 to 5 minutes. In a medium-size bowl, whisk together flour, baking powder, baking soda, salt, and cinnamon. Set aside. In a small bowl, whisk together buttermilk, eggs, and vanilla.

3. Add a third of the flour mixture to butter/sugar mixture and mix just to combine at medium-low speed. Add half the buttermilk mixture and mix just to combine. Repeat, adding another third of the flour mixture, then remaining buttermilk mixture, then remaining flour mixture.

4. Turn dough out onto a lightly floured surface and knead four times to bring it all together; then roll into an even cylinder about 18 inches long. Cut cylinder into six equal parts (each 3 inches long), then press each part into a disk, wrap in plastic, and refrigerate at least 30 minutes (up to a day).

5. Preheat the oven to 400° and set rack to middle position. On a lightly floured surface, roll out one disk to a 10-inch circle (use a bit more flour if it sticks). Using a cake pan as your guide, trim dough into a perfect 9-inch circle; then lay it in a pan to bake. Repeat with two more pieces.

6. Bake all three, rotating pans halfway through, until layers are lightly golden and just beginning to pull away from the sides, 10 to 12 minutes. Remove from the oven and cool on wire racks 10 minutes. Remove layers

(recipe continues on next page)

and set aside. When pans are cool, butter and flour them once more, and repeat rolling, cutting, and baking with the other three dough rounds.

7. Assemble the cake: Choose your prettiest, smoothest "top" layer and set it aside. Choose your bottom layer and use an offset spatula to spread about ⅓ cup cran-berry filling over the top, all the way to the edges. Top with another layer and another ⅓ cup filling. Repeat three more times, then top with the prettiest layer. Cover with plastic wrap and refrigerate at least 24 hours, preferably 48; then dust top with confectioners' sugar, cut into thin slices, and serve.

PINEAPPLE RIGHT-SIDE-UP CAKE

"My husband's godmother made this pineapple cake whenever we visited her in the Catskills," wrote reader Ruth M. Werner. *"We think of her whenever we make this easy, delicious dessert."*

TOTAL TIME: 2 HOURS • **HANDS-ON TIME:** 1 HOUR 30 MINUTES • **YIELD:** 8 TO 10 SERVINGS

FOR THE CAKE:
- Butter (for pans)
- 1 20-ounce can crushed pineapple in juice
- 2 cups all-purpose flour, plus more for pans
- 1¼ cups granulated sugar
- ¾ teaspoon table salt
- 1 teaspoon baking powder
- ½ teaspoon baking soda
- ½ cup vegetable oil
- ⅔ cup chopped toasted almonds
- 2 large eggs
- 1 teaspoon vanilla extract

FOR THE ICING:
- 1 8-ounce package light ("Neufchatel") cream cheese, at room temperature
- ½ cup (1 stick) salted butter, at room temperature
- 1½ cups confectioners' sugar
- 1 teaspoon vanilla extract
- Garnish: slivered almonds

1. Preheat the oven to 350° and set a rack to the middle position. Butter and flour two 8-inch cake pans. Pour pineapple into a strainer over a bowl. Press with a spatula (drink or discard juice); set aside.

2. In a large mixing bowl, whisk together flour, sugar, salt, baking powder, and baking soda. Add vegetable oil, almonds, eggs, vanilla, and drained pineapple. Beat until smooth. Pour into prepared cake pans and bake until top is nicely browned and a toothpick comes out clean, 35 to 45 minutes. Cool on wire racks to room temperature while you prepare the icing.

3. Clean out the mixing bowl; then add cream cheese and butter and beat together. Add sugar and vanilla. Beat until smooth. Chill until cake reaches room temperature. Ice the cake and sprinkle with almonds. Chill until ready to serve.

GERMAN STRAWBERRY CAKE

TOTAL TIME: 1 HOUR 20 MINUTES, PLUS COOLING • **HANDS-ON TIME:** 40 MINUTES • **YIELD:** 16 SLICES

FOR THE CAKE:

- 1½ **cups cake flour**
- 1 **tablespoon baking powder**
- ½ **teaspoon table salt, plus a pinch (for egg whites)**
- 4 **large eggs, separated**
- 1 **cup granulated sugar (extra-fine preferred)**
- 1 **teaspoon vanilla extract**
- ¾ **cup water**

FOR THE TOPPING:

- 2 **quarts fresh strawberries, divided**
- 2 **teaspoons cornstarch**
- ½ **cup sugar (optional)**
- 3 **tablespoons water (optional)**
 Garnish: 8–10 fresh strawberries

1. Preheat the oven to 325° and set a rack to the middle position.
2. In a small bowl, whisk together flour, baking powder, and salt; set aside. In a clean, dry bowl, beat the egg whites with a pinch of salt until firm (but not dry) peaks form; set aside.
3. In a large bowl, beat the egg yolks until thick and pale-colored. Gradually add sugar and continue beating. Add vanilla. While continuing to beat, alternately add water and flour mixture in 2 batches. Using a rubber spatula, gently fold in egg whites.
4. Pour into an ungreased, flat-bottomed 12-inch tube pan (don't use a Bundt pan) and bake for 40 to 45 minutes, or until lightly golden and a toothpick inserted into the center comes out clean.
5. Remove from the oven and immediately invert the pan upside down over the neck of a bottle. Let the cake cool completely before removing.
6. Next, make the topping: Set aside 8 to 10 of your best-looking berries for the garnish. Hull and halve the remaining berries and mash well. Strain the berries until you have ⅔ to 1 cup of juice, reserving pulp. Combine the juice with the cornstarch and boil for 5 minutes, stirring continuously. Remove from the heat. Hull the remaining 8 to 10 berries and arrange them on top of the cake. Pour the thickened strawberry juice over the berries.
7. The cake is delicious if you stop here, but if you like even more intense strawberry flavor, purée the strained strawberry pulp until smooth; then combine with ½ cup sugar and 3 tablespoons water and bring to a boil. Reduce heat and simmer 5 minutes, stirring continuously. Pour over the top of the cake. Chill at least 30 minutes and serve.

VERMONT SPICED CHOCOLATE POTATO CAKE

We know this recipe is very old, though we don't know its exact origin. Sweet cakes made with potatoes appear in traditional Acadian and Irish cooking, and the use of spices means this recipe was likely a 19th- century invention. The combination of mashed potato and chocolate makes for a fragrant, dense, moist cake that will have you thinking about the holidays.

TOTAL TIME: 1 HOUR 45 MINUTES • HANDS-ON TIME: 30 MINUTES • YIELD: 12 SLICES

2½   **cups all-purpose flour, sifted**
4   **teaspoons baking powder**
½   **teaspoon table salt**
½   **teaspoon ground cinnamon**
½   **teaspoon ground cloves**
¼   **teaspoon freshly grated nutmeg**
¼   **teaspoon ground allspice**
¾   **cup unsalted butter, softened**
2   **cups granulated sugar**
2   **squares unsweetened (baking) chocolate, melted**
1   **cup freshly mashed potato**
2   **large eggs, separated, at room temperature**
½   **teaspoon vanilla extract**
½   **teaspoon almond extract**
¾   **cup whole milk**
1   **cup chopped walnuts**
   Garnish: confectioners' sugar

1. Preheat the oven to 350° and grease a 10-inch tube or Bundt pan.
2. In a medium-size bowl, whisk together the flour, baking powder, salt, and spices. Set aside.
3. In a large bowl, cream the butter and sugar until light and fluffy. Add the melted chocolate and mashed potato, and beat until smooth. Add the egg yolks and extracts and continue beating.
4. Add the flour mixture alternately with the milk. Fold in the nuts. Set aside. In a clean, dry, medium-size bowl, beat the egg whites until firm but not dry; then gently fold into the batter.
5. Pour the batter into the prepared pan, and bake for 1 hour or until a knife inserted into the center comes out clean. Let cool for 15 minutes; then turn onto a wire rack to cool completely. Dust with confectioners' sugar before serving.

WELLESLEY FUDGE CAKE

There are several stories about the origins of this cake from Wellesley, Massachusetts. Some say it evolved from the batches of fudge made by young Wellesley College ladies studying the "domestic sciences," and was popularized around the turn of the last century. According to the book Ex Libris: A Treasury of Recipes from the Friends of the Wellesley Free Libraries, *the actual cake was first served at the Wellesley Tea Room, located over Parker's Shoe Store in Wellesley Square, and then later made its way to the Blue Dragon restaurant.*

TOTAL TIME: ABOUT 1 HOUR 30 MINUTES, PLUS COOLING • **HANDS-ON TIME:** 45 MINUTES • **YIELD:** 10 TO 12 SERVINGS

FOR THE CAKE:

- 4 squares (4 ounces) unsweetened (baking) chocolate
- ½ cup hot water
- 1¾ cups granulated sugar, divided
- 1¾ cups cake or all-purpose flour, plus more for pans
- 1 teaspoon baking soda
- 1 teaspoon table salt
- ½ cup salted butter, softened, plus more for pans
- 3 large eggs, at room temperature
- ⅔ cup buttermilk
- 1 teaspoon vanilla extract

FOR THE FROSTING:

- 4 squares (4 ounces) unsweetened (baking) chocolate
- 1½ cups milk
- 4 cups granulated sugar
- ¼ teaspoon table salt
- 4 teaspoons light corn syrup
- ¼ cup (½ stick) salted butter, softened
- 2 teaspoons vanilla extract

1. Preheat the oven to 350° and set a rack to the middle position. Grease and flour two 9-inch square or round cake pans.

2. Make the cake: Put the chocolate and hot water in the top of a double boiler over simmering water and cook, stirring occasionally, until chocolate melts. Add ½ cup sugar, stir, and cook for 2 minutes. Set aside and let cool to lukewarm.

3. In a medium-size bowl, whisk the flour, baking soda, and salt together; set aside. In another bowl, cream the butter with the remaining sugar until light and fluffy, about 4 minutes. Add the eggs, one at a time, beating thoroughly after each addition. Then alternately in add the flour mixture and the buttermilk, beating after each addition. Blend in the vanilla and the lukewarm chocolate mixture, and stir until evenly combined. Pour the batter into the two cake pans and bake until the cake springs back when lightly pressed, 30 to 35 minutes.

4. Meanwhile, make the frosting: Put chocolate and milk in a medium-size saucepan and set over low heat. Cook, stirring continuously, until chocolate melts. Add sugar, salt, and corn syrup, and stir until sugar dissolves. Increase heat to medium-low and cook, stirring, until mixture reaches 235° to 245° on a candy thermometer (soft ball stage). Remove from heat. Stir in butter and vanilla. Cool to lukewarm; then beat until creamy. When cake has cooled to room temperature, spread frosting between layers and over the top and sides.

BUTTERMILK PIE

In the Yankee spirit of "use it up," the rural housewife accumulated many recipes calling for buttermilk, the liquid that's left when butter is churned. Here, it lends unique flavor to a custard-like pie, brightened with lemon zest.

TOTAL TIME: 1 HOUR 20 MINUTES • **HANDS-ON TIME:** 20 MINUTES • **YIELD:** 8 SLICES

Single-crust pastry dough (see p. 180)
½ cup (1 stick) unsalted butter, softened
⅔ cup granulated sugar
3 large eggs
2 teaspoons vanilla extract
3 tablespoons all-purpose flour, plus more for pan
½ teaspoon table salt
Zest of ½ lemon
2 cups buttermilk

1. Preheat the oven to 400° and set a rack to the middle position. On a floured surface, roll out the chilled dough, working from the center, to a 10-inch circle. Carefully transfer the dough to a pie plate and press into the sides. Drape any excess crust over the edge; then fold under and crimp into a scalloped edge: Holding your right thumb and forefinger in a "U" shape; then poke the crust between them using your left forefinger. Use a fork to prick holes in the bottom of the dough. Line the dough with foil, and fill with dried beans or pie weights. Bake for 8 minutes. Carefully remove the weights and foil; then continue baking for another 5 minutes (the crust will still look pale). Remove from the oven and set aside.

2. In a large bowl, cream together the butter and sugar until light and fluffy. Add the eggs one at a time, beating thoroughly after each addition and scraping the sides of the bowl with a rubber spatula as necessary. Add the vanilla, flour, salt, and zest. Slowly beat in the buttermilk until thoroughly combined.

3. Pour the mixture into the prepared pie shell and bake for 10 minutes. Reduce heat to 325° and bake for an additional 45 to 50 minutes, or until the top is nicely browned and a knife inserted into the center comes out clean. Use a paper towel to gently wick away any excess moisture on the surface, and then transfer to a wire rack to cool. Best when served warm.

LEMON MERINGUE PIE
(recipe on opposite page)

LEMON MERINGUE PIE

A pie that's as pretty as it is delicious, the lemon meringue dates back to the mid-1800s. Lemon custards go back much further, as does meringue. But it took a few hundred years for them to meet in a pastry crust. Make this on a dry, cool day; meringue doesn't fare well in hot, humid weather.

TOTAL TIME: 1 HOUR PLUS AT LEAST 4 HOURS • **HANDS-ON TIME:** 45 MINUTES • **YIELD:** 8 SERVINGS

NOTE: *If you're uncomfortable using uncooked egg whites, look for pasteurized egg whites, available in the dairy case of many supermarkets.*

FOR THE FILLING:

	Flour (for work surface)
	Single-crust pastry dough (see p. 180)
1½	cups granulated sugar
1½	cups plus ⅓ cup water
½	teaspoon table salt
½	cup cornstarch
4	large egg yolks, lightly beaten
½	cup freshly squeezed lemon juice (from about 3 lemons)
3	tablespoons salted butter, cut into cubes
1	teaspoon freshly grated lemon zest

FOR THE MERINGUE:

4	egg whites (see "Note," above)
½	teaspoon cream of tartar
¼	teaspoon table salt
½	cup granulated sugar

1. Preheat the oven to 400° and set a rack to the middle position. On a floured surface, roll out the chilled dough, working from the center, to a 10-inch circle. Carefully transfer the dough to a pie plate and press into the sides. Drape any excess crust over the edge; then fold under and crimp into a scalloped edge: Hold your right thumb and forefinger in a "U" shape; then poke the crust between them using your left forefinger. Use a fork to prick holes in the bottom of the dough. Line the dough with foil, and fill with dried beans or pie weights. Bake 10 minutes. Carefully remove the weights and foil; then continue baking another 10 minutes (the crust will be light golden brown). Remove from the oven and set aside.

2. To make the filling, combine the sugar, 1½ cups water, and salt in the top of a double boiler over high heat. Bring to a simmer. Mix the cornstarch with the remaining ⅓ cup water and add to the sugar mixture slowly, stirring continuously. Cook until thickened and clear. Remove from the heat and cool 5 minutes. Stir in the egg yolks and lemon juice. Return the mixture to the heat and stir until it begins to bubble. Remove from the heat and stir in the butter and zest. Cover and cool until lukewarm.

3. To make the meringue, combine the egg whites, cream of tartar, and salt in a clean mixing bowl and beat until frothy. Gradually add the sugar, beating until glossy peaks form when you lift the beater.

4. Preheat the oven to 325°. Pour the filling into the pie shell. Pile on the meringue, spreading to the edge of the crust. Bake for 15 minutes, or until lightly browned. For a darker meringue, set it under the broiler, watching continuously, until it reaches the desired color, 1 to 2 minutes. Cool on a rack for 1 hour. Chill for at least 3 hours before serving. Best served the day it's made.

MARLBOROUGH PIE

Yankee senior lifestyle editor Amy Traverso developed this pie for her Apple Lover's Cookbook *(2011: W.W. Norton). She writes, "I always assumed this dish was a Massachusetts native, associating it with Boston's Marlborough Street, which is very posh and lined with 19th-century townhouses. I pictured some proper Bostonian's clever cook inventing an apple custard pie and serving it at a dinner attended by Fannie Farmer, who took it from there—never mind that the godmother of American cooking didn't travel in those circles. In reality, this custard pie filled with shredded apples and flavored with lemon and sherry goes back much further, first appearing in a 1660 British book,* The Accomplisht Cook, *written by a Paris-trained chef named Robert May. It traveled to the New World with the colonists and became popular in Massachusetts, where it was also called 'Deerfield Pie.'"*

TOTAL TIME: 2 HOURS • HANDS-ON TIME: 50 MINUTES • YIELD: 8 SERVINGS

Single-crust pastry dough (see p. 180)
- 2 large firm-tart apples, such as Granny Smith or Northern Spy (about 1 pound total), peeled and cored
- 2 large firm-sweet apples, such as Golden Delicious or Pink Lady (about 1 pound total), peeled and cored
- 3 tablespoons lemon juice
- 3 tablespoons dry sherry
- 2 tablespoons salted butter
- ⅔ cup granulated sugar
- 3 large eggs
- 1 cup light cream
- ¼ teaspoon ground cinnamon
- ¼ teaspoon freshly grated nutmeg
- ¼ teaspoon table salt
- Garnish: whipped cream (optional)

1. Preheat the oven to 400° and set a rack to the middle position. On a floured surface, roll out the chilled dough, working from the center, to a 10-inch circle. Carefully transfer the dough to a pie plate and press into the sides. Drape any excess crust over the edge; then fold under and crimp into a scalloped edge: Hold your right thumb and forefinger in a "U" shape; then poke the crust between them using your left forefinger. Use a fork to prick holes in the bottom of the dough. Line the dough with foil, and fill with dried beans or pie weights. Bake for 8 minutes. Carefully remove the weights and foil; then continue baking for another 5 minutes (the crust will still look pale). Remove from the oven and set aside.

2. Reduce the oven temperature to 350°. Using a box grater, grate the apples down to the core. Transfer to a medium-size bowl and stir in the lemon juice and sherry. In a large, heavy-bottomed skillet over medium-high heat, melt the butter; then add the apples (with their liquid) and the sugar, and cook, stirring, until the liquid begins to boil. Reduce the heat to a simmer; then continue cooking, stirring occasionally, until the apples are tender and most of the liquid evaporates, about 10 minutes. Remove from the heat and let cool for 10 minutes.

3. Meanwhile, in a large bowl, whisk together the eggs, cream, cinnamon, nutmeg, and salt. Stir in the apple mixture. Pour the filling into the crust; then bake until the custard is set but not browned, about 35 minutes. Let cool on a rack for 30 minutes; then serve warm or at room temperature, with whipped cream if you like.

**POPCORN BALLS,
NEVER-FAIL CHRISTMAS FUDGE,
CAPE COD SALTWATER TAFFY**
(recipes on pages 159, 159)

POPCORN BALLS

This old-time confection dates back to the mid-1800s and remains a favorite Halloween treat. The balls are easy to make. The only trick is to watch the caramel carefully: It can go from golden brown to nearly black in the matter just of a few seconds.

TOTAL TIME: 35 MINUTES • HANDS-ON TIME: 20 MINUTES • YIELD: 12 TO 15 BALLS

1 cup granulated sugar
½ cup light corn syrup
½ teaspoon white or cider vinegar
½ teaspoon table salt
¼ cup salted butter, plus more for bowl and hands
1 teaspoon vanilla extract
12 cups popped popcorn

1. Grease a large mixing bowl with butter or cooking spray.

2. In a heavy 3- to 4-quart saucepan, stir together sugar, corn syrup, vinegar, and salt. Bring to a boil over medium-high heat and stir in butter. Reduce heat to medium-low and boil gently until light golden brown, about 3 minutes, stirring often; then remove from heat and stir in vanilla.

3. Put popped corn in the large mixing bowl. Pour syrup mixture over the popcorn and stir with a spatula until popcorn is evenly coated. As soon as the mixture is cool enough to handle, butter your hands and shape the popcorn into 2- to 3-inch balls. When the balls are cool, wrap them in plastic or waxed paper.

CAPE COD SALTWATER TAFFY

Most people agree that saltwater taffy was first popularized at Fralinger's, a shop on the Atlantic City boardwalk, around 1883. It was never actually made with saltwater, though the recipe does call for some salt. According to the New York Times, *the name may simply refer to the boardwalk's proximity to the sea.*

TOTAL TIME: 1 HOUR • HANDS-ON TIME: 45 MINUTES • YIELD: 35 TO 40 PIECES

1¼ cups granulated sugar
4 teaspoons cornstarch
½ cup light corn syrup
½ cup water
1 tablespoon unsalted butter, plus more for baking sheets and hands
½ teaspoon table salt

2 teaspoons flavor extract (your choice of orange, lemon, strawberry, maple, etc.)
¼ teaspoon vanilla extract
Food coloring (your choice)

(recipe continues on next page)

1. Liberally grease a large baking sheet with butter and set aside.
2. In a medium-size saucepan, combine the sugar and cornstarch. Add the corn syrup, water, butter, and salt and stir over medium heat until the butter melts and the mixture comes to a boil.
3. Cook, without stirring, until the mixture just reaches 250° on a candy thermometer, or until a small piece dropped into a cup of cold water forms a firm, but not sticky, ball. Remove from the heat immediately and stir in flavoring, vanilla, and several drops of food coloring.
4. Pour the mixture onto the greased baking sheet and let cool until you can handle it, about 15 minutes.
5. Grease your hands with butter; then pull and stretch the taffy until it lightens in color, about 15 minutes total. Form into ropes and cut into pieces with buttered scissors. Wrap the pieces in squares of parchment or waxed paper.

NEVER-FAIL CHRISTMAS FUDGE

Even if you've never made candy before in your life, give this fudge a try. True to its name (and thanks to the presence of marshmallows), it won't seize or crumble or make you tear your hair out. The recipe comes from Priscilla Soule, a lifelong candymaker from Sangerville, Maine, and ran in Yankee's December 2001 issue. Come Christmastime in her family, "there were so many friends and relatives to pack boxes for that it seemed we were endlessly making fudge, bonbons, candied citrus, and sugarplums," she wrote. "We probably spent four or five days making holiday candy."

TOTAL TIME: 20 MINUTES PLUS 4 TO 6 HOURS COOLING • **HANDS-ON TIME:** 20 MINUTES • **YIELD:** 30 PIECES

2 **cups granulated sugar**
⅔ **cup evaporated milk**
12 **regular marshmallows (not minis)**
½ **cup unsalted butter, plus more for pan**
⅛ **teaspoon table salt**
1 **cup (8 ounces) semisweet chocolate chips**
1 **cup chopped walnuts**
1 **teaspoon pure vanilla extract**

1. Grease an 8-inch square pan or line it with nonstick foil. Set aside.
2. In a 2-quart saucepan over medium heat, combine the sugar, milk, marshmallows, butter, and salt. Cook, stirring continuously, until the mixture is bubbling.
3. Boil and stir for 5 minutes; remove from the heat. Stir in the chocolate chips until completely melted. Add the walnuts and vanilla.
4. Spread into the prepared pan and cool for 4 to 6 hours in the refrigerator before cutting.
5. Store in an airtight container in the refrigerator or at room temperature.

**DILLY BEANS,
MARJORIE'S GREEN TOMATO RELISH**
(recipes on pages 163, 162)

Preserves and Sauces

Pickles are back in vogue in this era of DIY everything; so are homemade sauces. We've selected a few choice recipes that are as easy to make as they are rewarding. Peach butter can be made overnight while you sleep. Green tomato relish is the solution to all your underripe end-of-season fruits. And dilly beans will turn you into a canning buff. But if you're looking for more immediate gratification, try our 10-minute hot fudge sauce or 5-minute homemade buttermilk dressing.

MARJORIE'S GREEN TOMATO RELISH

Here's the perfect solution for early-summer tomato cravings (or for those end-of-season fruits that don't ripen before the frost). For prettiest results, use a variety of colorful bell peppers: orange, yellow, purple, red, and green. If you'd like a little heat, add a jalapeño or two.

TOTAL TIME: 3 HOURS 15 MINUTES • **HANDS-ON TIME:** 55 MINUTES • **YIELD:** 6 PINTS

NOTE: *If you're pressed for time, you can pulse the vegetables in a food processor until they're chopped into ¼-inch pieces. Dicing the vegetables by hand takes more time, but it makes the relish look extra pretty.*

24	medium-large green tomatoes
4	large white, yellow, or sweet onions
6	medium-large bell peppers, preferably a mix of colors
1–2	jalapeño peppers (optional)
3	tablespoons pickling salt
3	cups granulated sugar
3	tablespoons mixed pickling spices, tied in a cloth
3	cups white distilled vinegar

1. Finely dice (see "Note," left) the tomatoes, onions, peppers, and jalapeños (if using).
2. Transfer the vegetables to a large bowl, stir in the pickling salt, and let stand for 1 hour. Drain and discard liquid; then add the sugar, pickling spices, and vinegar. Transfer mixture to a 4-quart pot and set it over high heat; bring to a boil. Lower heat to low and simmer gently for 1 hour.
3. Pack the relish into hot, fully sterilized pint jars, leaving a quarter-inch of head space at the top. Remove any air bubbles by tapping the jars lightly; wipe jar rims with a clean towel. Cover at once with metal lids, and screw on bands. Seal and process for 5 minutes in a boiling-water bath. Cool and store in a cool, dry place.

DILLY BEANS

In 1960, Time *magazine noted a new snack that had commandeered the cocktail party circuit: "Rarely has the discerning palate been assailed by a less pretentious offering: a raw string bean, pickled in vinegar and dill. Yet the Dilly Bean had captured the fancy of cocktail-hour nibblers on the East and West coasts and was rapidly making tycoons out of two ex-schoolmarms who run Manhattan's Park & Hagna Inc. People also serve Dilly Beans in martinis, salads, sandwiches, cream cheese, and beef Stroganoff—and have discovered that poodles love them." The "ex-schoolmarms" were two savvy young New Jersey teachers named Sonya Hagna and Jacquelyn Park, who'd come up with the formula and were selling the beans to specialty markets in New York. They eventually left the classroom, and their beans went on to national fame. Properly canned, these tart, crunchy dilled beans will keep for months—the perfect holiday or housewarming gift.*

TOTAL TIME: 1 HOUR 10 MINUTES • HANDS-ON TIME: 45 MINUTES • YIELD: 4 PINTS

2	pounds fresh green beans, stems removed
8–10	sprigs fresh dill
4	medium-size cloves garlic, sliced lengthwise
4	cups cider vinegar (5% acidity)
2	cups water
3	tablespoons coarse or pickling salt
1½	teaspoons fennel seeds
1	teaspoon hot red-pepper flakes

1. Wash beans; then cut into lengths ½ inch shorter than your jar. Fill a 3- to 4-quart pot with enough water to cover the beans by an inch. Set pot over high heat, bring to a boil, and cook just 1½ minutes. Drain, then plunge into ice water to stop cooking; drain. Pack beans tightly into fully sterilized jars. Add 2 or 3 sprigs of dill and a few slices of garlic to each jar.

2. Add vinegar, water, salt, fennel, and flakes to the pot. Over high heat, bring mixture to a boil. Boil 1 minute; then pour over beans, filling each jar to ½ inch from top. Remove air bubbles by tapping jars lightly; wipe rims with a clean towel. Cover at once with metal lids, and screw on bands. Process in a boiling-water bath for 15 minutes.

WATERCRESS SAUCE

Remember when watercress was the go-to peppery green for salads? That was before the 1990s, when it was muscled out of the top slot by arugula. Meanwhile, the use of boiled eggs in sauces goes back centuries—the ancient Egyptians recorded recipes for sauces that were bound or thickened with eggs, as this one is. And so these two classics come together in a sauce that makes a perfect accompaniment to grilled or roasted fish, shrimp, or chicken.

TOTAL TIME: 15 MINUTES • HANDS-ON TIME: 15 MINUTES • YIELD: ABOUT 1½ CUPS

3 large eggs
1 bunch watercress, roughly chopped
2 tablespoons olive oil
Juice of 2 lemons
½ teaspoon kosher or sea salt
¼ teaspoon freshly ground black pepper

1. Bring a medium-size pot of water to boil over high heat. Add eggs, cover, and reduce heat to low. Cook exactly 5 minutes; then remove eggs and plunge into cold water.
2. When eggs are cool enough to handle, carefully peel them and put them in a blender. Add the watercress, olive oil, lemon juice, and seasonings, and blend until smooth. Refrigerate until ready to serve.

PEACH BUTTER

You may be familiar with this recipe's better-known cousin, apple butter, all well and good. But here's the truth of the matter: Nothing captures the essence of late summer more than this sweet-tart preserve. It cooks down to a silky brown purée, but tastes only of sunshine and nectar.

TOTAL TIME: 8 TO 10 HOURS • HANDS-ON TIME: 25 MINUTES • YIELD: ABOUT 6 CUPS (3 PINTS)

8 pounds fresh ripe peaches
2⅔ cups granulated sugar
½ cup freshly squeezed orange juice
4 cinnamon sticks
½ teaspoon kosher or sea salt

1. Using a sharp knife, score each peach with a shallow X shape on the bottom. Fill a large pot (at least 5 quarts) with water and bring to a boil over high heat. Add peaches and boil until skins loosen, about 1 minute. Remove peaches from water with a slotted spoon and run under cold water to stop cooking. Peaches should now slip easily out of their skins. Discard skins.
2. Using a knife or your hands, break peaches up into large pieces and put into a 6-quart slow cooker; discard the pits. Add sugar, orange juice, cinnamon sticks, and salt, and stir. Set heat to high and cover; cook until mixture is simmering, 1 to 1½ hours. Reduce heat to low and leave lid slightly ajar. Cook until peach butter is thick and mahogany-colored, 7 to 9 hours. Pour into sterilized jars, seal, and process 10 minutes in a boiling-water bath.

GREEN GODDESS SALAD DRESSING

Said to have been President Eisenhower's favorite dressing, this concoction turns a green salad into a work of art. Add tuna fish, poached chicken, and grilled bread to make a light meal.

TOTAL TIME: 15 MINUTES PLUS AT LEAST 30 MINUTES CHILLING • HANDS-ON TIME: 15 MINUTES • YIELD: ABOUT 1¾ CUPS

1 cup mayonnaise	1. Combine all ingredients in a blender and pulse until smooth. Cover and chill at least 30 minutes to let flavors combine. Store in the refrigerator for up to 10 days.
½ cup sour cream	
1 clove garlic, smashed	
2 tablespoons minced scallions (green onions)	
2 tablespoons white wine vinegar or tarragon vinegar	
1 tablespoon anchovy paste	
2 teaspoons lemon juice	
¼ teaspoon freshly ground black pepper	

BUTTERMILK RANCH DRESSING

In 1954 a pair of young Nebraskans headed west to open a 120-acre dude ranch near Santa Barbara, California; they called it "Hidden Valley Ranch." Steve and Gayle Henson welcomed visitors for hiking, horseback riding, and fishing and served hearty American fare at night. Their homemade buttermilk salad dressing became so popular that guests began buying it by the bottle—and thus the ranch-dressing craze was born. This is our take on the classic recipe.

TOTAL TIME: 15 MINUTES • HANDS-ON TIME: 15 MINUTES • YIELD: ABOUT 1¾ CUPS

1 cup buttermilk	1. In a small bowl, whisk together all ingredients. Serve immediately, or cover and chill up to 1 week.
½ cup mayonnaise	
2 teaspoons fresh lemon juice	
1 tablespoon minced fresh cilantro	
1 tablespoon minced fresh chives	
½ teaspoon kosher or sea salt	
¼ teaspoon mustard powder	
⅛ teaspoon freshly ground black pepper	

GRAPE CATSUP

"When I was a teenager in New Hampshire in the 1950s, we had a Concord grapevine that grew on the side of the woodshed," wrote Yankee *reader Lucille Mitchell in our September 1999 issue. "In the fall, my mother picked the large purple grapes and made grape catsup. Its spicy aroma filled the house and tickled our appetites. It made an excellent addition when served with meat and fowl. The thought of it brings to my mind fall's crisp, cool days and hills of beautiful foliage. I am now old and a long way from home, and these are the things I miss."*

TOTAL TIME: 2 HOURS 30 MINUTES • HANDS-ON TIME: 40 MINUTES • YIELD: ABOUT 1½ QUARTS

4 **pounds Concord grapes**
2 **pounds granulated sugar**
2 **cups white or cider vinegar**
1 **tablespoon ground cinnamon**
1 **tablespoon ground allspice**
2 **teaspoons ground cloves**

1. Combine ingredients in a large (4- to 5-quart) heavy-bottomed pot over high heat and bring to a boil. Reduce heat to low and gently simmer until grapes cook down and juice thickens, about 1 hour 45 minutes. Pass through a strainer to remove seeds and skins. Pour catsup into sterilized jars, seal, and process 10 minutes in a boiling-water bath.

TARTAR SAUCE

Tartar sauce is the necessary accompaniment to fried fish. It's not clear why the sauce was named after the 5th-century Turkic-speaking Tatar people of Mongolia—it's certainly not part of their traditional cuisine. But recipes for sauces made from mayonnaise and capers or pickles date back to the 19th century.

This particular recipe is from Chickie Angelakis, proprietor of The Clam Box, a mecca of fried-clamdom located in Ipswich, Massachusetts.

TOTAL TIME: 10 MINUTES • HANDS-ON TIME: 10 MINUTES • YIELD: ¾ CUP

½ **cup mayonnaise**
¼ **cup sweet relish, drained**
1 **tablespoon minced sweet onion**

1. Stir ingredients together in a small bowl. Let sit 10 minutes before serving to let the flavors combine.

**MARJORIE'S GREEN TOMATO RELISH,
GRAPE CATSUP, PEACH BUTTER**
(recipes opposite and on pages 162, 164)

LEMON BUTTER

"In our family, lemon butter was made and eaten on Easter Sunday," recalled Yankee *reader Jane Dahlgren in our April 2000 issue. "No one knows why we had it only on Easter. My grandmother, Emma Spear, who was born in 1897, remembered having lemon butter on Easter as a young girl. Her grandmother made it, so the recipe and stories have been passed down through the generations . . . [It's] really more of a lemon sauce. As children, my brother and I loved it, but as we got older and low-fat low-sugar recipes became the vogue, we shunned it as "too fattening." We'd always eat a little to be polite, but our family noted our lack of enthusiasm. Then, in her old age, my grandmother became a diabetic. She could no longer eat lemon butter, and because none of us insisted on it, she stopped making it. But I've decided I miss this family tradition. This Easter I'll make lemon butter. I know my grandmother would approve, and I hope my children enjoy it as much as I did."*

TOTAL TIME: 20 MINUTES • **HANDS-ON TIME:** 20 MINUTES • **YIELD:** 1 SCANT QUART

2 **large eggs**
2 **cups plus 3 tablespoons water, divided**
1½ **cups granulated sugar**
 Juice and grated zest of 2 large lemons
4 **tablespoons salted butter**
2 **tablespoons cornstarch**

1. Beat eggs well; then beat in 2 cups water, sugar, and lemon. Place in a heavy, nonreactive saucepan over low flame and add butter. Cook, stirring frequently, until slightly thickened (don't let it boil).
2. Dissolve cornstarch in remaining 3 tablespoons water. Add this mixture to the sauce, and continue to cook and stir until sauce coats the spoon thickly. Serve chilled.

BUTTERSCOTCH SAUCE

Technically, butterscotch is a hard candy, a variation on toffee that dates back to the early 19th century. Over time, the term has come to describe sauces, ice creams, and puddings that feature brown sugar and butter as the primary flavors.

TOTAL TIME: 15 MINUTES • **HANDS-ON TIME:** 15 MINUTES • **YIELD:** 3 CUPS

¾ **cup firmly packed light-brown sugar**
1 **cup corn syrup**
¼ **cup (½ stick) salted butter**
1 **cup light cream**
¼ **teaspoon table salt**

1. In a 2- to 3-quart saucepan over medium-high heat, bring the brown sugar, corn syrup, and butter to a simmer, stirring continuously. Simmer about 5 minutes; then add the cream and salt and bring back to a simmer. Cook 3 more minutes, stirring all the while. Serve hot or cold.

IRENE'S FUDGE SAUCE

Here's another item from Yankee's *former "Recipe with a History" column. Dorene Lengyel of Lynnfield, Massachusetts, sent it to us in 1996 with the following story: "In the early 1950s it was tradition in our home for my mother to put a big roast in the oven Sunday mornings before church. Following the service she served the family a grand full-course Sunday dinner. After all the preparation and cleanup, she felt supper should be easy. So in the early evening my father would drive to the Brigham's in Winchester or Medford Square to buy vanilla ice cream and a package of salted pecans while my mother made her famous fudge sauce. Every Sunday evening we ate sundaes while watching* The Ed Sullivan Show *on our seven-inch TV with a magnifying screen in front of it. Now my family eats a sandwich for Sunday [lunch], makes homemade pizza for supper, and watches a video or golf match on TV. Occasionally we have ice cream, Mother's warm fudge sauce, and salted nuts for dessert." For Dorene's mother, this sauce was her vacation from cooking. It's that easy—and delicious.*

TOTAL TIME: 12 MINUTES • **HANDS-ON TIME:** 12 MINUTES • **YIELD:** ABOUT 1 CUP

½ cup granulated sugar

1 teaspoon cornstarch

¼ teaspoon table salt

2 ounces unsweetened (baking) chocolate

6 tablespoons milk

3 tablespoons salted butter

1 teaspoon vanilla extract

1. In a small bowl, whisk together sugar, cornstarch, and salt. Set aside.

2. In a 2- to 3-quart saucepan, melt chocolate with milk and butter over medium-low heat. Simmer 3 minutes; then whisk in dry ingredients and cook, stirring, for 5 minutes. Mixture will thicken and become smooth and glossy. Turn the heat off and add vanilla. Serve warm.

SPICY RUM PUNCH, CRANBERRY CORDIAL
(recipes on pages 172, 173)

ONE-WEEK GINGER BEER
(recipe on opposite page)

TOM COLLINS FOR FOUR

This refreshing late-1800s cocktail from Old New York is a perfect summer sipper for a group.

TOTAL TIME: 10 MINUTES • **HANDS-ON TIME:** 10 MINUTES • **YIELD:** 4 SERVINGS

¼ **cup granulated sugar**
¼ **cup water**
8 **ounces dry gin**
8 **ounces freshly squeezed lemon juice**
    (from 3 to 4 lemons)
  Soda water
  Garnish: 4 lemon slices

1. Put sugar and water in a small saucepan over high heat and stir until sugar dissolves to make a syrup. Remove from heat.
2. Fill 4 tall glasses with ice. Into each, pour 2 ounces gin, 2 ounces lemon juice, and 1 to 2 teaspoons of the sugar syrup, depending on your taste. Top glass with soda water and stir. Garnish with lemon slices.

SIDECAR FOR ONE

The Ritz-Carlton in Paris lays claim to this sweet-tart cocktail, which first appeared during World War I, but other experts say it was created in London. Whatever its origins, it is timeless and elegant, a great drink to have in your bartending repertoire.

TOTAL TIME: 3 MINUTES • **HANDS-ON TIME:** 3 MINUTES • **YIELD:** 1 SERVING

4 **ounces brandy or cognac**
½ **ounce Cointreau**
½ **ounce freshly squeezed lemon juice**
  Garnishes: granulated sugar, lemon rind

1. Fill a cocktail shaker halfway with ice. Add the ingredients and shake well, at least 30 seconds. Pour into a chilled cocktail glass rimmed with sugar, and garnish with a twist of lemon rind.

TOM & JERRY

This holiday drink, a variation on eggnog made with brandy, was invented by a British sportswriter and journalist named Pierce Egan in the 1820s; it's named after two characters in his best-known satirical work, Life in London. *If you make the recipe in quantity, use a punch bowl and cups. Punch sets from the 1960s with "Tom & Jerry" written on them sometimes turn up at antiques shops and flea markets.*

TOTAL TIME: 35 MINUTES • **HANDS-ON TIME:** 35 MINUTES • **YIELD:** 4 SERVINGS

NOTE: *Use only fresh eggs from a reliable source in this recipe. If contamination is a concern, look for pasteurized eggs at your grocery store.*

- 2 **large eggs, separated**
- 1 **tablespoon granulated sugar**
- ½ **teaspoon ground allspice**
- 3 **tablespoons (1½ ounces) light rum**
- 3 **tablespoons (1½ ounces) brandy**
- ⅛ **teaspoon cream of tartar**
- 1⅓ **cups hot milk**
  Whole nutmeg (for grating)

1. Beat egg yolks, sugar, and allspice at high speed with an electric mixer until thick and lemon-colored. Blend in rum and brandy.
2. In separate mixing bowl, beat egg whites and cream of tartar until they form firm (but not dry) peaks. Fold in yolk mixture. Spoon ½ cup of the mixture into each of four warmed 8-ounce mugs. Fill each with ⅓ cup hot milk. Grate a bit of nutmeg on top and serve immediately.

**LEMON MERINGUE PIE,
SINGLE-CRUST PASTRY DOUGH**
(recipes on pages 155, 180)

Reference

SINGLE-CRUST PASTRY DOUGH

1 ¼ cups all-purpose flour, plus extra for work surface
1   tablespoon granulated sugar
½   teaspoon kosher or sea salt
9   tablespoons (1⅛ sticks) chilled unsalted butter,
      cut into small cubes
3–4   tablespoons ice water

1. In a medium-size bowl, whisk together flour, sugar, and salt until well combined.
2. Sprinkle butter over flour mixture, and use your fingers to work it in (rub your thumb against your fingertips, smearing the butter as you do). Stop when the mixture looks like cornmeal, with some pea-size bits of butter remaining.
3. Sprinkle 3 tablespoons ice water on top, and stir with a fork until dough begins to come together. If needed, add another tablespoon ice water.
4. Turn out onto a lightly floured surface and knead three times, or just enough to make a cohesive dough—don't overmix! (See p. 181, bottom.)
5. Gather into a ball; then press into a disk and wrap in plastic. Refrigerate 30 minutes.

DOUBLE-CRUST PASTRY DOUGH

2 ½ cups all-purpose flour, plus extra for work surface
2   tablespoons granulated sugar
1   teaspoon kosher or sea salt
18   tablespoons (2 ¼ sticks) chilled unsalted butter,
      cut into small cubes
6–8   tablespoons ice water

1. In a medium-size bowl, whisk together flour, sugar, and salt until well combined.
2. Sprinkle butter over flour mixture, and use your fingers to work it in (rub your thumb against your fingertips, smearing the butter as you do). Stop when the mixture looks like cornmeal, with some pea-size bits of butter remaining.
3. Sprinkle 6 tablespoons ice water on top, and stir with a fork until dough begins to come together. If needed, add more ice water, a tablespoon at a time.
4. Turn out onto a lightly floured surface and knead three times, or just enough to make a cohesive dough—don't overmix! (See p. 181, bottom.)
5. Gather into a ball; then divide into two pieces, one slightly larger than the other. Press each piece into a disk and wrap in plastic. Refrigerate 30 minutes.

THE WELL-TEMPERED EGG

If you've ever made a custard, a pudding, or an egg-based sauce or soup, you've probably had to "temper" the eggs by slowly adding a hot liquid to them, whisking all the while, in order to bring their temperature up more gradually. Why the extra step?

If you've ever made scrambled eggs, you've seen what happens when eggs are suddenly exposed to high heat: They firm up and coagulate. At very high heat, they become rubbery. Tempering avoids this problem in several ways. First, bringing the temperature up slowly will protect the eggs from immediate curdling. Second, it also dilutes the eggs and redistributes their proteins. As you stir in the hot liquid, the tightly coiled proteins unwind and break apart from one another, then reconnect in long strands, forming an invisible "mesh" that holds the liquid and eventually thickens into a beautiful custard sauce or soup.

COLD BUTTER & A LIGHT HAND:
THE SECRET TO PERFECT BISCUITS & PASTRY

You may have noticed that recipes for piecrust, scones, and biscuits usually tell you to keep your butter chilled and to "work quickly" when adding it to the dough. They also tend to warn against overmixing. These instructions aren't designed to make you nervous, though that's often the unintended consequence. Instead, they're meant to teach you the right technique.

Let's start with the butter: You don't want it to melt into the dough before baking. Why? Because when bits of butter melt in the heat of the oven, they release little bursts of steam that puff up a biscuit and make flaky layers in a piecrust. If they melt before baking, you lose the steam effect.

As for overmixing, the problem there is that it makes pastries tough. Flour contains a protein called *gluten* (familiar to most of us now because of gluten allergies), which is activated when it combines with water, milk, or other liquids. Gluten holds dough together with its rubber-band-like strands—which is good—but too much will yield a chewy texture. You do want that in bread, but you don't want that in your biscuits or pie. The more you mix the dough, the more gluten develops (that's why we knead our bread dough). So use a light hand for biscuits and pastry: Mix only as needed to form an uneven but cohesive dough.

COMMON HOUSEHOLD MEASURES

3 teaspoons = 1 tablespoon
16 tablespoons = 1 cup
1 cup = 8 ounces
2 cups = 1 pint
2 pints = 1 quart
4 quarts = 1 gallon

METRIC CONVERSIONS

½ teaspoon = 2 mL
1 teaspoon = 5 mL
1 tablespoon = 15 mL
¼ cup = 60 mL
⅓ cup = 75 mL
½ cup = 125 mL
⅔ cup = 150 mL
¾ cup = 175 mL
1 cup = 250 mL
1 liter = 1.057 U.S. liquid quarts
1 U.S. liquid quart = 0.946 liter
1 U.S. liquid gallon = 3.78 liters
1 gram = 0.035 ounce
1 ounce = 28.349 grams
1 kilogram = 2.2 pounds
1 pound = 0.45 kilogram

TEMPERATURE CONVERSIONS

- **To convert Fahrenheit to Celsius, subtract 32 from the Fahrenheit number, multiply by 5, and divide by 9.**

MEASURING VEGETABLES

Asparagus:
1 pound = 3 cups chopped

Beans (string):
1 pound = 4 cups chopped

Beets:
1 pound (5 medium) =
2½ cups chopped

Broccoli:
½ pound = 6 cups chopped

Cabbage:
1 pound = 4½ cups shredded

Carrots:
1 pound = 3½ cups sliced or grated

Celery:
1 pound = 4 cups chopped

Cucumbers:
1 pound (2 medium) = 4 cups sliced

Eggplant:
1 pound = 4 cups chopped =
2 cups cooked

Garlic:
1 clove = 1 teaspoon chopped

Leeks:
1 pound = 4 cups chopped =
2 cups cooked

Mushrooms:
1 pound = 5 to 6 cups sliced =
2 cups cooked

Onions:
1 pound = 4 cups sliced =
2 cups cooked

Parsnips:
1 pound unpeeled =
1½ cups cooked, puréed

Peas:
1 pound whole =
1–1½ cups shelled

Potatoes:
1 pound (3 medium) sliced =
2 cups mashed

Pumpkin:
1 pound = 4 cups chopped =
2 cups cooked and drained

Spinach:
1 pound = ¾–1 cup cooked

Squashes (summer):
1 pound = 4 cups grated =
2 cups sliced and cooked

Squashes (winter):
2 pounds = 2½ cups cooked, puréed

Sweet potatoes:
1 pound = 4 cups grated =
1 cup cooked, puréed

Swiss chard:
1 pound = 5–6 cups packed leaves =
1–1½ cups cooked

Tomatoes:
1 pound (3 or 4 medium) =
1½ cups seeded pulp

Turnips:
1 pound = 4 cups chopped =
2 cups cooked, mashed

MEASURING FRUIT

Apples:
1 pound (3 or 4 medium) =
3 cups sliced

Bananas:
1 pound (3 or 4 medium) =
1¾ cups mashed

Berries:
1 quart = 3½ cups

Dates:
1 pound = 2½ cups pitted

Lemons:
1 whole = 1–3 tablespoons juice;
1–1½ teaspoons grated rind

Limes:
1 whole = 1½–2 tablespoons juice

Oranges:
1 medium = 6–8 tablespoons juice;
2–3 tablespoons grated rind

Peaches:
1 pound (4 medium) = 3 cups sliced

Pears:
1 pound (4 medium) = 2 cups sliced

Rhubarb:
1 pound = 2 cups cooked

Strawberries:
1 quart = 3 cups sliced

Adapted with permission from *The Old Farmer's Almanac Garden-Fresh Cookbook* © 2011 by Yankee Publishing Inc.

SUBSTITUTIONS FOR COMMON INGREDIENTS

ITEM	QUANTITY	SUBSTITUTION
Allspice	1 teaspoon	½ teaspoon cinnamon plus ⅛ teaspoon ground cloves
Baking powder	1 teaspoon	¼ teaspoon baking soda plus ⅝ teaspoon cream of tartar
Breadcrumbs, dry	¼ cup	1 slice bread
Breadcrumbs, soft	½ cup	1 slice bread
Buttermilk	1 cup	1 cup plain yogurt
Chocolate, unsweetened	1 ounce	3 tablespoons cocoa plus 1 tablespoon butter or fat
Cream, heavy	1 cup	¾ cup milk plus ⅓ cup melted butter (won't whip)
Cream, light	1 cup	⅞ cup milk plus 3 tablespoons melted butter
Cream, sour	1 cup	⅞ cup buttermilk or plain yogurt plus 3 tablespoons melted butter
Flour, cake	1 cup	1 cup minus 2 tablespoons sifted all-purpose flour
Herbs, dried	½–1 teaspoon	1 tablespoon fresh, minced and packed
Lemon	1	1–3 tablespoons juice plus 1–1½ teaspoons grated rind
Mustard, prepared	1 tablespoon	1 teaspoon ground mustard
Tomato purée	1 cup	½ cup tomato paste plus ½ cup water
Vanilla	1-inch bean	1 teaspoon vanilla extract
Vinegar, balsamic	1 tablespoon	1 tablespoon red-wine vinegar plus ½ teaspoon sugar
Yeast	1 cake (⅗ ounce)	1 package (¼ ounce) dry active yeast
Yogurt, plain	1 cup	1 cup buttermilk

Adapted with permission from *The Old Farmer's Almanac Garden-Fresh Cookbook* © 2011 by Yankee Publishing Inc.

PAN SIZES & EQUIVALENTS

You may substitute one pan size for another, but the cooking time may change. For example, if a recipe calls for using an 8-inch round cake pan and baking 25 minutes but you use a 9-inch pan, the cake may bake in only 20 minutes because the batter forms a thinner layer in the larger pan. Also, specialty pans such as tube and Bundt pans distribute heat differently. Results may vary if you substitute a regular cake pan for a specialty one, even if the volume is the same. Here's a plan for those times when the correct-size pan is unavailable:

PAN SIZE	VOLUME	PAN SUBSTITUTE
9 x 1¼-inch pie pan	4 cups	8 x 1½-inch round cake pan
8½ x 4½ x 2½-inch loaf pan	6 cups 11 x 7 x 2-inch cake pan	four 5 x 2¼ x 2-inch loaf pans
9 x 5 x 3-inch loaf pan	8 cups 9 x 2-inch round cake pan	8 x 8 x 2-inch cake pan
15½ x 10½ x 1-inch jellyroll pan	10 cups two 8 x 2-inch round cake pans 9 x 2½-inch springform pan	9 x 9 x 2-inch cake pan
10 x 3½-inch Bundt pan	12 cups 9 x 3-inch tube pan 9 x 3-inch springform pan	two 8½ x 4½ x 2½-inch loaf pans
13 x 9 x 2-inch cake pan	14–15 cups two 8 x 8 x 2-inch cake pans	two 9 x 2-inch round cake pans

■ If the correct-size casserole is unavailable, substitute a baking pan. Again, think about the depth of the ingredients in the dish and lengthen or shorten the baking time accordingly.

CASSEROLE SIZE	VOLUME	PAN SUBSTITUTE
1½ quarts	6 cups	8½ x 4½ x 2½-inch loaf pan
2 quarts	8 cups	8 x 8 x 2-inch cake pan
2½ quarts	10 cups	9 x 9 x 2-inch cake pan
3 quarts	12 cups	13 x 9 x 2-inch cake pan
4 quarts	16 cups	14 x 10 x 2-inch cake pan

Adapted with permission from *The Old Farmer's Almanac Garden-Fresh Cookbook* © **2011 by Yankee Publishing Inc.**

Index

LOST AND VINTAGE RECIPES

Reference

Notes

Notes